To Mummy +
did you get my message?
(it was good eh! :D) Come and
check on me xxxx x 10000

From Jolie

:) I ♥ you 2

Taking Control
By Anthea Lawrence

The How & Why of Basic Gundog Training
(For any variety gundog)

© Copyright 2006 Anthea K. Lawrence.
All rights reserved. No part of this publication may be reproduced, stored in a retrieval system, or transmitted, in any form or by any means, electronic, mechanical, photocopying, recording, or otherwise, without the written prior permission of the author.

Note for Librarians: A cataloguing record for this book is available from Library and Archives Canada at www.collectionscanada.ca/amicus/index-e.html
ISBN 1-4120-9942-0

The photographs on the front cover and title page, show the late Mr Roger Smith and his Golden Retriever Courtridge Chantilly (Lily, to her friends)

TRAFFORD
PUBLISHING

Offices in Canada, USA, Ireland and UK

Book sales for North America and international:
Trafford Publishing, 6E–2333 Government St.,
Victoria, BC V8T 4P4 CANADA
phone 250 383 6864 (toll-free 1 888 232 4444)
fax 250 383 6804; email to orders@trafford.com
Book sales in Europe:
Trafford Publishing (UK) Limited, 9 Park End Street, 2nd Floor
Oxford, UK OX1 1HH UNITED KINGDOM
phone +44 (0)1865 722 113 (local rate 0845 230 9601)
facsimile +44 (0)1865 722 868; info.uk@trafford.com
Order online at:
trafford.com/06-1699

10 9 8 7 6 5 4 3 2

Acknowledgements

A special thank you to the following:

For the use of photographs;

> Richard Ashdown
> Mick Downes
> Paul Lawrence
> Paul Rawlings
> Keith Robinson
> Brian Smith
> Mary Ward
> Tony Ward

For help with reading and checking;

> Mick Downes
> Nigel Haines
> Alexis Prosser
> Mary Ward
> Tony Ward

I am indebted to the entire Ward Family for their help:

> Chris Ward and his company team for help in deciding on a title for the book;
>
> Keith and Sam Robinson, for use of their photographs and for trying some of the exercises with their new pack member, Seamus;
>
> Tony Ward, for his constructive criticism and Mary Ward, who has helped me get to this stage by her friendship, support, keeping

me reasonably sane, and her practical assistance in making sure all the exercises and tips worked, *no matter what*.....

My thanks and love to you all.

Dedication

For Gemma (Mistybrook Breeze of Courtridge)

Many thanks to Richard Ashdown who enabled me to have this latest, delightful, addition to our domestic pack.

Contents

Introduction

1. Commands	1 - 6
2. Getting started	9 – 17
Flow Chart 1	18
3. Heelwork	21 - 34
4. Sit	35 - 43
5. Hold and Give commands	45 - 54
6. Developing work on heelwork & sits	57 - 71
7. Water experience	78 - 82
8. Leave it command	86 - 95
9. Steadiness	96 - 102
10. Noise and Gunshot	103 – 111
Flow Chart 2	112
11. Testing the understanding of heel and sit	114 - 126
12. Recall	129 - 137
13. Going for walks and free play	140 - 147
14. Get over command	149 - 153
15. Developing work on hold and give commands	156 - 163
16. Whistle	164 – 170
Flow Chart 3	171
17. Marked retrieve	172 - 180
18. Developing work with water	182 - 191
19. The go back command	192 - 200
20. The get on command	201 - 208
21. Blinds	209 - 218
22. Development of directional work	221 - 232
23. Conclusion	233 – 236

Photographs

(a) & (b) Heelwork – getting started	7 – 8
(c) & (d) Heelwork – the aim	19 – 20
(e) Young puppies and 'holding'	44
(f) & (g) Working on steadiness	55 – 56
(h), (i), (j) & (k) Taking control of exit and entry to the car	72 – 75
(l) & (m) Water experience	76 – 77
(n) Exploring water on a water training course	83
(o) & (p) The 'leave it' command	84 – 85
(q) Gates and doorways	113
(r) & (s) Concentration – common faults	127 – 128
(t) & (u) Playing	138 – 139
(v) The 'get over' command	148
(w) & (x) Teaching the 'hold'	154 – 155
(y) Water work	181
(z) Hand signals	219 – 220

Introduction

This is a book about basic gundog training, aimed at those people who wish to train a puppy themselves either on their own or in conjunction with some gundog training classes. It is for people of all levels of experience and ability, those new to training, or for those who have trained one or numerous dogs in the past, perhaps using different methods.

It is a foundation course, where all gundogs should start, no matter what the aspirations of the owner/handler in terms of the hoped for future. It is therefore suitable for those who aspire to competition work in Field Trials and Gundog Working Tests; for show bred dogs whose owners wish to attempt a Show Gundog Working Certificate (SGWC) in order to attain the status of Champion; for those wishing to achieve a Kennel Club Working Gundog Certificate (WGC); and for all those people who have a gundog breed puppy wishing to develop the potential and/or help to give the dog a more fulfilled and interesting life through channelling the dog's natural abilities in a constructive way.

The methods used are kind, reward based with praise and, unlike the majority of similar training books, this book is designed to help people concerning the training needs of a puppy from 8 weeks old, with more formal training starting at around 10 to 12 weeks of age.

Most training books concerning gundogs continue with the long-held view that gundogs should not begin their training until approximately 6 months of age or older, and although the outdated belief in dog-breaking has largely disappeared from the language of such books, the principles of this are still very much in evidence. This is demonstrated quite clearly by many trainers who believe in allowing dogs to learn and develop many different facets of behaviour, which are undesirable in a trained adult gundog. These undesirable facets then have to be eradicated when formal training starts.

Although the often harsh methods of doing this have now largely disappeared, the sad fact remains that these dogs have been encouraged to behave in a way which is not desirable. Training methods are therefore punishment based and dogs learn by doing something wrong, being punished and therefore having to do something again and again, until they happen to discover the one action which is not punished.

Unfortunately the old dog breaking techniques have now been replaced, by some trainers, with breaking by the use of electric collars. These devices, euphemistically called 'remote trainers' or 'electronic training aids' have, in my opinion, no place in training a dog. They are a form of abuse which should have no place in a society which should have the rights of animals as part of the consideration in terms of how animals are treated in all respects.

In my view, it is kinder, and so much easier to teach a dog from the beginning, how to behave properly and in ways which will not change for the rest of its life.

Many people wishing to train a gundog puppy themselves, instead of sending a puppy away to be trained, at approximately 6 months of age, by a professional trainer have problems: in that they sometimes do not have the skills to be learner and teacher to their dog at the same time; do not have the expertise to know what to do when things go wrong or things don't work out successfully for them or they cannot get the results achieved by professional trainers. Books on training can be useful, but readers are given no help, in the majority of books, in terms of why certain facets are necessary, or how to do many of the basics which are almost forgotten in the race to get out into the shooting field or into Field Trials.

Training a gundog should concern training a dog to be a useful companion in the shooting field.

This book started out as small training leaflets which were given out at classes to help new handlers with the concepts involved to explain the *how* part of teaching a dog as well as the *why* the training is needed. The leaflets have simply grown in number and content.

An over-riding feature in my methods is that of having control over a dog at all times hence the title *'Taking Control'*. The sub-title brings in my reasons for producing the original training leaflets in that people needed to know *how* to do something coupled with the reason behind it. The reason, or the *why,* not only helps in understanding but also motivates and gives goals, hence *'The How & Why of Basic Gundog Training'*.

Training a dog should be enjoyable both for trainee and the handler.

Training a dog is a hobby in its own right and although some people may have numerous goals at the start of training, what they want to do with the training, what they want to achieve etc. an equal number of people simply go training and it is the training class or session, the taking part, the achievements gained in each step of training, which is their motivation and joy.

Whatever your motivation may be, whatever your goals and aspirations you will have responsibilities as soon as you decide to have, buy and bring home a young gundog puppy. There is a tremendous amount of information available concerning every breed of gundog from Breed Clubs, general gundog clubs, Field Trial societies, and the Kennel Club. Choose wisely and with care and then begin the task of bringing the new arrival up correctly.

If you choose my methods of training, you will start teaching your puppy what is required of him for life, right from the moment he enters your door and has his first wee on your kitchen floor! Love him, care for him and remember that loving and caring is also about educating, praising and sometimes disciplining. All these things must blend together.

I still feel the magic of special moments when I and my dog are working together. To many people those moments may seem unremarkable. They are moments not connected with award-winning Field Trials or anything which others may see as a measure or mark of success. Sitting on the bank of a river at dusk in the middle of December may seem a poor setting for magic moments but I have had them in plenty.

Hearing a duck shot, seeing it fall into a fast flowing, major river. Watching my dog sitting, shivering on the bank with me, knowing he too has seen the duck but is waiting, quivering in anticipation, for his special word of command which means 'joy of joy, I can leap into the river, swim and get that duck for my master, my leader.'

Watching my dog battling against the current, how he turns into a current and lines himself up, treading water, so as not to miss the fast travelling duck which is coming towards him – that is magic, because I have not taught him how to do that. I have taught him what he needs to do to obey me, but on top of that he has brought his own unique set of skills which he uses just for me. Yes he is getting something out of it as well, but when a tired dog is prepared to go into a freezing, cold, river time after time and goes when I command him so to do, it is hard to imagine he is getting too much joy other than in his desire to please me.

Those moments are the ones to treasure and I hope all of you will have similar moments which will make up your treasure chest of magical moments.

It is quite a frightening process when you start for the first time or begin again, with a new puppy. It is also fun and exciting, a time of joyful anticipation and hard work but an experience I would not choose to miss. I wish everyone every success at the start of this journey on which they are about to embark and I hope that some of what you are about to read, will work for you and give you and your dog a life-time partnership full of happiness.

Anthea Lawrence

CHAPTER ONE

Commands.

Commands are the words and groups of words to which people attach a meaning. A dog does not speak our language and therefore we need to keep crucial command words to a minimum, keep words as simple as we can and have only one word to mean one specific action. A command should, once the dog has learned its meaning, alert the dog and allow him to switch onto certain key words which he will know he has to obey.

It is the sound the word makes which is important and the actual word we choose to use, that is the meaning we choose to attach to a word, is largely irrelevant as long as we are consistent in attaching the same meaning to any particular word. In theory, we can teach a dog that when we say 'Sit' we mean 'lie down'; when we say 'Stand' we mean 'sit' and when we say 'Go' we mean 'come'.

In practice however, this tends to get difficult, not due to the dog, but due to the handler being unable to remember what action they meant by a specific word. It is also more desirable to have words which are understood by other people, particularly judges if one wishes to compete, as well as having words which are as unique in sound as possible. Gundog trainers, handlers, and instructors therefore tend to use similar words, with a few variations. In this way, when a handler gives a specific command to a dog a judge would be expecting the dog to perform a specific action.

Here is a list of verbal commands and the meaning, which I use in training. If there are any commands listed here which you already use but which you have taught your dog to mean some action other than the meaning listed, you will need to find a different word for that particular meaning.

Heel.	Be on my left hand side, 6 inches away, with your right shoulder parallel with my left leg.
Sit.	Put your bottom on the ground.
Hold.	Take an item into your mouth and keep it in your mouth, no matter what happens, until I take hold of the item and say 'give'.
Give.	When I hold an item which is in your mouth and say 'give', you must release the item immediately.
Leave it	Dismiss from your mind all thought of having or doing what you are thinking of taking possession of, or getting involved in.
Come	Return to me as quickly as you can.
Get Over	Negotiate and get to the other side of *any* obstacle directly in front of you.
Name of dog	Used in specific circumstances only, and which will mean: Go and retrieve a mark, when nothing else has happened in between the mark being thrown and the dog being sent
Go Back	Go away from me in a straight line.
Get On	Go in a straight line to the left or right, depending on which arm I use.
Hie Lost	Search and hunt the area approximately 6 feet in diameter from where you are.
Shake	You may now get rid of the water in your coat
Off you go	The release command: you can stop obeying the last command I gave you. You are free to go off on your own.

There are other commands which I tend to use later in training but which perhaps are not strictly necessary with all dogs. I include them here so that if you need to select some words for yourself as commands, you can avoid any which may be needed later.

- Get in. Physically enter dense cover
- Look up. Search high up, rather than on the ground. This is used when a bird is perhaps caught up in branches.
- Gone away. Whatever the dog was interested in, has gone. This is used for puppies when toys are put away but also used for older dogs when perhaps pursuing a wounded bird which gets up and flies away.

In addition to verbal commands there are also commands with the whistle and commands by hand signal.

Whistle:

- 1 toot: Sit and/or stop and look at me, because I am going to give you another command and/or help you. (Often called the 'stop' whistle)
- Several short, quick toots: This is a recall and the meaning is the same as 'Come'
- Several short but slower toots: I use this as a different type of recall and it means: come towards me, as I am going to give you another command and/or help you. Many people use this whistle command as a hunting command instead of a 'come towards me' command. It cannot be used as both.

Hand signals:

Only one hand at a time is ever used to command a dog and a hand is often a helping command used in conjunction with a verbal and/or whistle command.

One hand held up in the air above the head, is used as a 'sit' command and is similar to the 1 toot whistle command above. It is usually used only at a distance in conjunction with the whistle and either hand may be used.

The following, are for directional guidance and are used after a 'sit' whistle and hand signal:

- 🐾 'Get on' command. It should be remembered that the dog is facing the handler for this command, which means right to the handler is left to the dog. The left hand is used, with the arm out at 90° from the body, with a verbal 'get on' command to indicate that the dog should go out to its right. Similarly, the right hand is used with the arm out at 90° from the body, with a verbal 'get on' command to indicate that the dog should go out to its left.
- 🐾 'Go back' command. It should be remembered for this command, that although the dog is facing the handler waiting for the command, in order to obey the command, he must turn round and face in the same direction as the handler. Right to the handler will therefore also be right to the dog, when he has turned round. A hand and arm, brought up from its normal position to above the handler's head is used in conjunction with a verbal 'go back' command. If the dog is to go away slightly left the left hand and arm is used and if the dog is to go away slightly right, the right hand is used.
- 🐾 'Come towards me' command. It should be remembered that the dog is facing the handler for this command, which means right to the handler is left to the dog. A right hand and arm pointing downwards (at a 20 past the hour) used in conjunction with a recall, 'come towards me' whistle, is used to bring the dog forward slightly to its left. Similarly a left hand and arm pointing downwards (20 to the hour) used in conjunction with a recall 'come towards me' whistle, is used to bring the dog forward and slightly to its right.

Use of commands.

It is important that a dog learns to obey the first and only command given to initiate any action or position. In order for this to happen, handlers need to discipline themselves and only *give* one command.

The benefit in using a positioning and praise type of training method is that giving one command is more easily achieved because the command word is given once, and then the handler shows the dog what he must do to obey.

Once the dog is obeying a command, that is once the dog is in the required position or is taking the appropriate action, *then* the command word can be used as often as necessary whilst that particular command continues to be obeyed.

The repetition of a command word is used only as a reminder to the dog to continue obeying you and it is an important part of training using this method. Puppies and older dogs, just beginning training, have a very short attention span and are unable to keep in their minds for much longer than a few seconds what they are supposed to be doing. Reminder commands are therefore essential to enable the learning process to proceed in a satisfactory manner. Reminder commands prevent, or help to prevent, the dog disobeying in perhaps the second or two after they have been helped to understand the meaning of what you want. Because a dog forgets and perhaps moves, some handlers feel their dog is deliberately trying to annoy them or the dog is stupid or wilful. The handler therefore wants to get into a punishing mode or get angry with the dog instead of continuing to teach the dog with patience what it is that is required of him. Usually it is simply that the dog has forgotten, yes in two seconds, what he was supposed to be doing.

At the start of training, when a dog is being taught, he needs reminders and these reminder commands, together with praise, are saying to him, 'yes, you are doing the right thing by continuing to do what you are doing and I am pleased with you.' Later on in training many of these reminder commands will be dropped because you will build into the training longer periods when the dog will have to remember what he should be doing or risk your displeasure, but that is for later.

In the beginning it is much better to remind the dog almost continuously so that he does not go wrong and he will learn far more from this because he will remain in position and gain useful information about what you are trying to teach him. Handlers who give the most reminder commands, together with praise, have dogs which are much steadier. They also have dogs which appear to learn what is required of them, concerning basic commands, in a shorter time. Handlers who do not give reminder commands and who give insufficient praise have dogs which are constantly moving, unable to grasp what they should do, and appear in a state of confusion.

The above two statements have very little to do with the dogs!

Some novice handlers get confused about how and when to use commands. This gets easier as time goes on but meanwhile, if handlers are confused, they will give confusing messages to their dogs and it takes longer for the dogs to learn what is required. The statement to remember is:

'Give one command to initiate some action and then give as many reminder commands as you can give, with praise, to encourage the dog to continue what he is doing'.

(a) Heelwork – getting started.
The first few training sessions should concentrate on teaching the 'heel' and the 'sit' commands. Practice needs to be on an individual basis but also, when possible, in the company of other dogs and handlers.

(Photograph: Keith Robinson)

(Photograph: Mary Ward)

(b)
Working alone, or working in a group the emphasis must be on concentrating on what each handler is trying to teach their dog.

(Photographs: Mary & Tony Ward)

The pictures show an Irish Red Setter of 4months and a litter group of Goldens aged 12 weeks.

CHAPTER TWO

Getting started

The first stage of training will cover teaching the commands 'Heel' and 'Sit'.

These are two simple commands but they are the foundations upon which everything else is built and are the basis of taking control of your dog. These two commands may, to a novice handler, appear to be very little to do with gundog training but without them, nothing can be achieved and with them, everything can be achieved. These two commands are so important – if you do not believe this statement: just imagine if you are able to, the result if every dog in the world obeyed, every time, instantly, these two commands. Every time the handler said 'heel' the dog walked to heel, every time a handler said 'sit' the dog sat and every dog went on obeying each command no matter what else was happening around it. There would be few problems with dogs, every dog would be under control and every handler would have control.

The words heel and sit are the words I use and you need to decide for yourself which words you will use and then use these precise words for the life-time of your dog.

I shall use the above words throughout.

If you want a dog who responds quickly, accurately and happily to every command you give him it is vital that you, the handler, learn to react quickly to every situation. Your reactions and responses are vital in teaching the dog what you want and the quicker your responses, the quicker the dog will learn. You need to make things easy for yourself and the dog, so don't over complicate things; try not to teach more than one new thing at a time and don't move onto something else until your dog is happy and confident with the first thing you are teaching. All dogs learn at different rates and training is not a race but should be a continual learning process for all concerned.

You must learn how to discipline yourself and to begin with this usually means **being consistent**.

You need to discipline yourself particularly regarding commands. Dogs must respond to the first and only command you give for a particular action and handlers therefore need to give only one command right from the start of training. If 'sit' means to the dog 'put your bottom on the ground' then that is what must happen if the dog is told 'sit'. If a handler says 'sit' and then just stands and looks at the dog and the dog does nothing many handlers repeat the 'sit' command and the dog still does nothing. By the time the, by now very angry, handler gets to the sixth 'sit' command, the sound of the command has not only got very much louder, but has changed out of all recognition from the sound the original command made. The command, to the dog therefore becomes:

'Sit, sit, sit, sit, sit, sit'. It is only on the last, loudest word that the handler galvanizes into action and 'helps' the dog, usually by grabbing the dog and pushing his bottom on the ground. This type of behaviour by a handler is seen as a punishment by the dog and it is unjust. This is not training and is certainly no way to teach a dog all he needs to know, and certainly not how a dog learns to maintain his respect for the handler, his leader!

It is a difficult task for those new to dog training; they have to learn things themselves whilst at the same time teaching their dog. They are pupil and teacher simultaneously, but it is the only way you can do it, so the first lesson for the handler is to remember:

- **Give only one command, in the same tone of voice, every time.**
- **Show the dog what he must do by positioning him correctly.**

☻ **Praise him, and smile whilst you are doing it.**

A dog needs to know (a) what he must do to obey a command but he also needs to know (b) when he must obey. The positioning method of training teaches the dog both of these factors at the same time. The dog learns because he is unable to go wrong: the positioning shows him the *what* and the fact that the handler positions him immediately after the command is given, shows him the *when*, which is now, immediately he hears the first command. The dog then gets his rewards, which are a warm smile and a 'good boy'.

Positioning means that the handler physically puts the dog in the required position. I give a command, for example 'sit' and immediately bend down and put the dog in position. I then praise by saying 'good boy/girl' in a pleasant but ordinary tone of voice. The sequence is therefore, command, position, praise. All over and done with in seconds and after a few sessions of following this exact pattern the dog knows what is expected when the command is given.

Once I have taught a dog what he is expected to do when I give a command, and I know he has learnt the lesson, I will introduce a punishment if he does not obey the command. Before you die of fright, let me explain: I do not believe in physical punishment of a dog and I neither use punishment of this type nor allow punishment like this to be used by anyone in my classes. Most dogs want to know how to obey and most dogs actually want to obey. All they lack, on occasions is a good leader to teach them. I believe in teaching and praise to allow a dog to learn; however, praise (the reward) is like one side of a coin and the other side of the coin is punishment. Although the reverse of the coin may not show itself frequently, it is there, and should be used appropriately.

My punishment is a growl.

I teach dogs my language in showing them what action they should take when I say a particular word. I also make use of their language.

All dogs, even very young puppies, understand what a growl means. They know a growl means they are doing something which the other dog does not like and as the other dog is bigger and/or stronger and/or more superior than they are, they had better stop that behaviour or else!

So when it becomes necessary, that is when I know the dog understands what to do to obey me, but chooses not to obey me, I use a growl. The sequence therefore would become; command, dog does not obey, growl, put the dog in position, then praise.

I always praise a dog for being correct, even if I have had to chastise them in some way and have had to put them in position because it must be remembered that the emphasis has to be on the teaching. The tools to teach a dog are: commands, demonstrating, praising when the dog gets it right, punishing when the dog disobeys. After any disobedience and punishment however, the handler must give the dog the opportunity to learn from it, by demonstrating again what the dog should do and by praising the correct action.

Do not be in too much of a hurry to get away from being the teacher, into being the disciplinarian. Some dogs need a long time being taught what to do before they understand they must do something when commanded, whereas many handlers want to get away from what they are teaching and move onto something else and therefore get away from teaching into punishing, far too quickly. So take your time.

My message to the dog, if I could explain in words, is: 'I will teach you with a lot of kindness and patience, what I expect you to do when I say a certain word, which is a command. When you obey that command, whether by yourself or with me helping you, I will praise you and I will leave you in no doubt that you have done the right thing. Once I am sure that I have taught you what you should do when I give that command, I expect instant obedience. If you do not obey instantly I will punish you by growling and I will then show you again what I expect you to do. I will then praise you.'

In the same way as the need to teach a dog an action for a particular command, the only way to show the dog the philosophy, is by the actions of the handler.

The lessons for the handler are therefore as follows:

- **Always use the same tone of voice every time you give a command, and never change your tone of voice for a command.**
- **Never give a command word more than once to initiate action by the dog or yourself.**
- **If you have to get cross – growl. (Getting cross should always be acted and never a reality emotion for the handler)**
- **Never say command words in a cross voice; use other words with which to communicate your displeasure if you have to say something! I'm sure you'll be able to think of some but many handlers use the word 'No' or 'Enough'.**
- **Use the warmest, happiest voice you have to praise. The bigger gap you can have in the range of tone between your warm, praising voice and your loud cross growl, the better. The voice scale to aim for is:**

Warm praise   Commands   **Horrible growl**

Training and work programme.

I am frequently asked, 'when should I start training my dog?' and my answer is, 'as soon as you get him home to live with you'.

Many years ago it was always the done thing to wait until a dog was at least 6 months old before any training was given (and some people continue with this belief) and frequently a dog had learned all manner of inappropriate behaviour in that period. Consequently the early stages of training were frequently spent in trying to undo many aspects of a dog's behaviour which were undesirable before any constructive work could be done concerning the desirable. This was called 'dog breaking' because the dog had to be broken of its bad habits and depending on; the trainer, the temperament of the dog and the habits accrued by the dog, this type of training was sometimes quite harsh.

Young puppies are at the height of their learning capacity when they are under 6 months of age. This is the period when in the wild, they would be learning everything they need to know; to survive in the dog pack as individuals and to play their part as a member of the pack for the benefit of the whole pack. I see no reason why, if we are bringing a dog home to join our domestic pack, we should not begin to teach a puppy all he needs to know to take his place within our pack. I therefore believe in training beginning immediately I bring a puppy home at 8 weeks or so. Of course this is not formal gundog training as such but it is nevertheless, training. The puppy is learning, with guidance, how he should behave in his new environment.

In general I like to give the puppy a few weeks in the home and garden when he is learning things concerning domestic arrangements: where he is to sleep, where he is to go for toileting, when he will be fed, what he can play with, where he will be confined when necessary, where he is allowed to wander freely and what the specific noises in our household mean. A puppy must have time to be a puppy, but simultaneously, he is learning what is allowed and what is not allowed. This all has to be managed with the safety and welfare of the puppy in mind, but also has to take account of one crucial factor in particular; that is, a puppy should not be allowed to develop habits which later will be seen as undesirable and this is the responsibility of the adult humans in the household.

During this period of domestic learning, there are some specific groups of words which should be introduced so that a puppy will begin to understand their meaning. These are not commands in the way a 'sit' command can be taught by showing the dog what to do, so they take time for a puppy to learn.

- The dog's name. Everyone wants their dog to understand who he is but caution should be taken in terms of how often the dog's name is used. You should also take care not to use the dog's name to mean a specific action. It is surprising how many messages a human can convey, just by saying a dog's name in a certain way and used too much the name alone can start to mean: come here, go away, get on the chair, get off the sofa or stop doing that. Use it sparingly and try not to convey any meaning other than the fact that the particular word is who the dog is. It is only humans which need to call a dog something. I feel that dogs really do not need a name apart from convenience for their owner.
- A toileting phrase. Every time a puppy squats to urinate or defecate, put a word to the action. I use 'be quick'. The choice of words is entirely up to you but you should choose something you could use in public! Having a dog which will urinate on command later on in life, is very useful.
- A release command. This is a word which releases the puppy from the last command you gave him. Obviously to begin, the puppy does not know any commands but it is useful to begin this when you take the puppy out into the garden for example. I use the words 'OK off you go'. You should choose your own words. This release command will be needed later but now is the time to begin the understanding.

Formal training in terms of a puppy learning what will be required of him, concerning obedience to specific commands, can usually be started at around 10 weeks of age and this is the age when I will first put a lead on a puppy and he will have his first proper lesson as opposed to learning things which I have enabled him to learn around the house and parts of the garden.

Your first few days of training should consist of one short, (5 to 10 minutes) training session and on occasions, several similar length sessions per day. You will find dogs work better just before they are fed, so try and aim for a training session prior to meals rather than straight after a meal. For very young puppies, timing of small training sessions is important. You need to aim for one of their active periods prior to a meal. There is no point in trying to train and teach a puppy when it has either a full tummy or is tired and needs to sleep. As the puppy grows, this will be less of a problem, but it is always best to train before, rather than straight after, meal times. (This is true for handlers as well as dogs!)

It is a good idea to write down what you intend to do in a training session, go out and do it, and then write down afterwards what you achieved and what you will do for your next session. Monitor your progress as you are going along. At the start, always do your training at the same location. Once your dog is beginning to make a bit of progress, then you need to go to different locations and try the same things. Go back to your first location again when you are introducing something new to teach the dog. In this way the dog learns to do a certain thing in one place and then learns he must do that particular thing in other and all places. The advantage too, is that the first location ceases to be very exciting for the dog and he will concentrate that much better. Most people find that their own garden is the ideal place to start training or to use certainly in the first few weeks.

You can gradually increase the length of time for your training sessions as you begin to have more things to do but it is still better to have several short bursts in one day rather than try to put it all together and try to do an hour. If you can't manage any training for a day or two, or even longer due to a holiday, don't try and make up for the time you have lost, by trying to do too much but simply revise up to the point you had reached before the break. Provided you and the puppy have retained everything learned then continue as though there has been no gap.

Don't be in too much of a rush to get through the first stages of training as these are the basics, the foundations on which you will build the rest of your training and the rest of your life together with your dog. As with all foundations, if they are not constructed correctly, you will find that all subsequent training may tumble down or may disintegrate due to a lack of attention at the right time. People often encounter problems later and the solution to problems never lies at the point where the problem occurs but will be much further back. This means you have to stop and go back several days or weeks or months. Getting the foundations right, pays off later, however long this takes.

When you have had a few sessions with your dog, try and join up with a friend or join a training class so you can do some training with others and your dog gets used to working with you whilst ignoring other people and dogs.

When the time is right for you and your puppy, you should begin with heelwork and you should try and do this on your own with the puppy and not in front of an audience or in a place with lots of distractions.

Good luck and try to enjoy yourself. In this way your puppy will love being with you and you will enjoy being with your puppy.

Today should be the start of you *Taking Control* and the start of your puppy relaxing when he senses that someone *is* in control. He expects fair leadership; he expects to be taught what is required of him to survive in his new pack. Don't disappoint him!

Flow chart (1) - for the first stage of training.

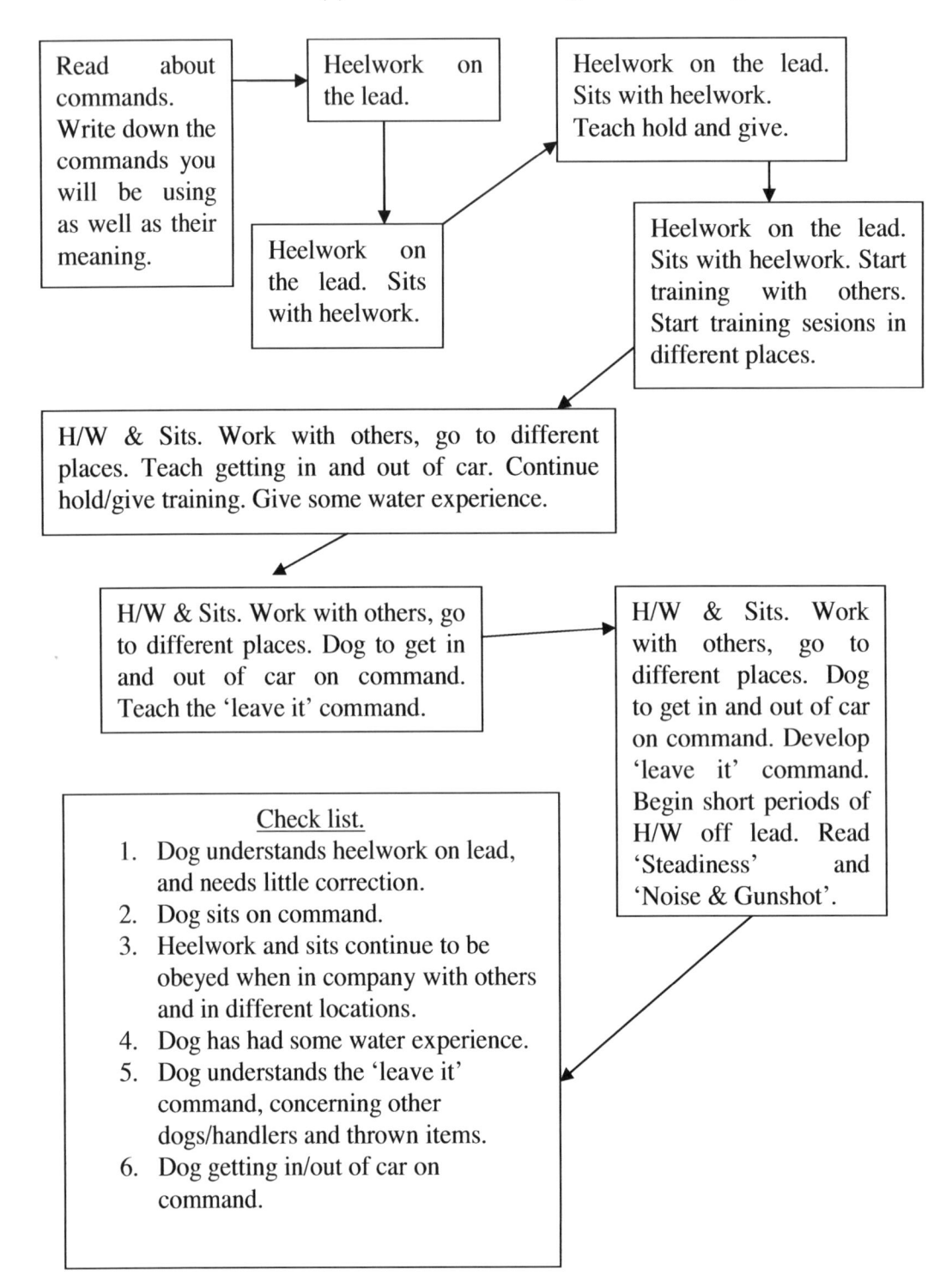

Read about commands. Write down the commands you will be using as well as their meaning.	→	Heelwork on the lead.

Heelwork on the lead. → Heelwork on the lead. Sits with heelwork.

Heelwork on the lead. Sits with heelwork. Teach hold and give.

↓

Heelwork on the lead. Sits with heelwork. Start training with others. Start training sesions in different places.

↓

H/W & Sits. Work with others, go to different places. Teach getting in and out of car. Continue hold/give training. Give some water experience.

↓

H/W & Sits. Work with others, go to different places. Dog to get in and out of car on command. Teach the 'leave it' command.

→ H/W & Sits. Work with others, go to different places. Dog to get in and out of car on command. Develop 'leave it' command. Begin short periods of H/W off lead. Read 'Steadiness' and 'Noise & Gunshot'.

Check list.
1. Dog understands heelwork on lead, and needs little correction.
2. Dog sits on command.
3. Heelwork and sits continue to be obeyed when in company with others and in different locations.
4. Dog has had some water experience.
5. Dog understands the 'leave it' command, concerning other dogs/handlers and thrown items.
6. Dog getting in/out of car on command.

Taking Control — 19 —

❧ (b) Heelwork – the aim

(Photograph: Brian Smith)

The correct heel position for a gundog

(d)

(Photograph: Mick Downes)

Working with other people and dogs in a training class when aspects of heelwork, sit and steadiness are combined with some retrieving

CHAPTER THREE

Heelwork

The purpose of teaching a gundog heelwork is to ensure that you have a well-behaved dog by your side, off the lead, on a shoot day. By 'well behaved', I mean simply that the dog will stay by your side whether you are walking, standing, sitting or whatever, and no matter what happens around him the dog will remain by your side unless he is commanded to do something else. **This is called having a 'steady dog'.**

For shoot purposes, having a well behaved dog is essential from a safety point of view, but it also helps to ensure a more pleasant and relaxed day not only for the handler of the dog but for all other participants.

If the handler is shooting, the dog is known as a 'peg dog', which means the dog sits at the peg with the person who is shooting (called the gun). The 'peg' is the numbered stake in the ground, which is allocated to the gun. At the start of the shoot the guns draw peg numbers, usually 1 – 8 or however many guns are shooting that day. The guns will move on after each drive perhaps 2 peg numbers so if a gun, for example drew peg number 3 at the start he will stand at peg 3 for the first drive, peg 5 for the second drive, peg 7 for the third drive, and so on.

The peg dog is required to retrieve birds shot by that gun. Usually the gun will wait until the end of a drive before sending his dog to retrieve the birds he has shot. Sometimes a dog will be sent in the middle of a drive however to retrieve a wounded bird that is not dead (called a runner).

If you do not shoot but have a partner or friend who shoots, you and your dog could gain some valuable experience by standing next to a gun and being a peg dog handler for the gun. (This will be at a much later date, of course once your dog has reached a satisfactory level of training).

Other jobs on a shoot day for handlers and dogs are 'beating' and 'picking –up'. The beaters and their dogs are responsible for driving and flushing the birds from such things as woods or cover crops towards the guns.

Usually the retriever breeds do not beat and if you want to compete with a retriever it is probably better to keep away from beating. Some people manage to do both but I believe it takes a lot of experience and training to combine the two successfully, mainly because beating requires the dog to be out in front of the handler seeking out birds and this can make a dog unsteady if the dog is needed more for retrieving and will have to sit and wait for longer periods whilst a drive is taking place or walk in the heel position for considerable time on a rough or walked-up shoot.

Most people opt for a picking-up job, particularly with a retrieving breed, as this gives handlers and dogs the opportunity to obtain experience on game and give the retriever breeds the opportunity to work on the job for which they were bred. The breed of gundog is possibly less important than the type of training given and Spaniels, HPR's and crossbred gundogs all seem to be able to cope with a picking-up role provided that steadiness and retrieving aspects of training have been taught adequately.

Depending on the individual shoot, the pickers-up and their dogs are not usually close to the guns. They are usually located well back behind the guns and they are responsible first of all for picking up (retrieving) any and all wounded birds during the drive and then for picking up any other birds which have been shot. On some occasions, for example Partridge shoots, wildfowling and particular drives on Pheasant and duck shoots, or if walking up, there may be a requirement for handlers and dogs to be much closer or in line with the guns with dogs off lead. This requires total steadiness and close heelwork.

Training.

To begin teaching heelwork you need to decide which command you are going to use. That is, which word you are going to use to attach to the specific action and position for your dog. I use the word 'heel'. You must decide for yourself which word you will use but I will use the word heel throughout.

The Definition of the heel command to the dog is: 'Be on my left hand side, 6 inches away, with your right shoulder level with my left leg.'

This definition is for the handler to understand initially. The dog will only come to understand the definition by associating the position, which the handler makes him adopt, with the repetition of the word. There is no point in just saying the word 'heel' to the dog if you then walk and let the dog walk in any position he feels like. If you say the word 'heel' and set off walking, the dog must walk in the position described in the definition otherwise you are teaching the dog that 'heel' means something other than your definition.

The answer therefore is to ensure that once you have said 'heel', you do not allow the dog to be in any position other than that described in the definition, without doing something about it in terms of correcting the dog and teaching him where he should be to earn his praise. You are, after all, the pack leader and as leader you have responsibilities to ensure that you teach correctly and that your dog understands the rules.

To start heelwork training the dog needs to be on a lead. Use a gundog slip lead and do not have a collar on the dog. The slip lead, when worn correctly, can tighten and loosen quickly without hurting the dog, but will act as a useful training aid for when he is out of position. It is important for this lead to be put onto the dog correctly. The correct way for a slip lead to be placed onto the dog is as follows:

- Hold onto the ring and lead with your left hand with the holding loop hanging downwards on the left.
- This then produces a loop of lead on the right, which will go over the dog's head.
- This loop will be straight on the top edge and curved downwards on the bottom edge. The straight edge will lie across the top of the dog's neck and the curved part of the loop will be round the throat and curving down to the chest.
- Standing in front of the dog, this loop can be placed over the dog's head.
- If there is a leather stop attached, the stop can then be moved to a position on the lead which ensures the lead cannot be slipped off, but is not tight round the dog's throat. There should be no restriction to stop the lead slipping appropriately to tighten, if necessary, but most importantly, to loosen.

Taking Control

> Diagram showing the correct way to put on the lead. The loop should be put onto the dog in this way, when facing the dog.

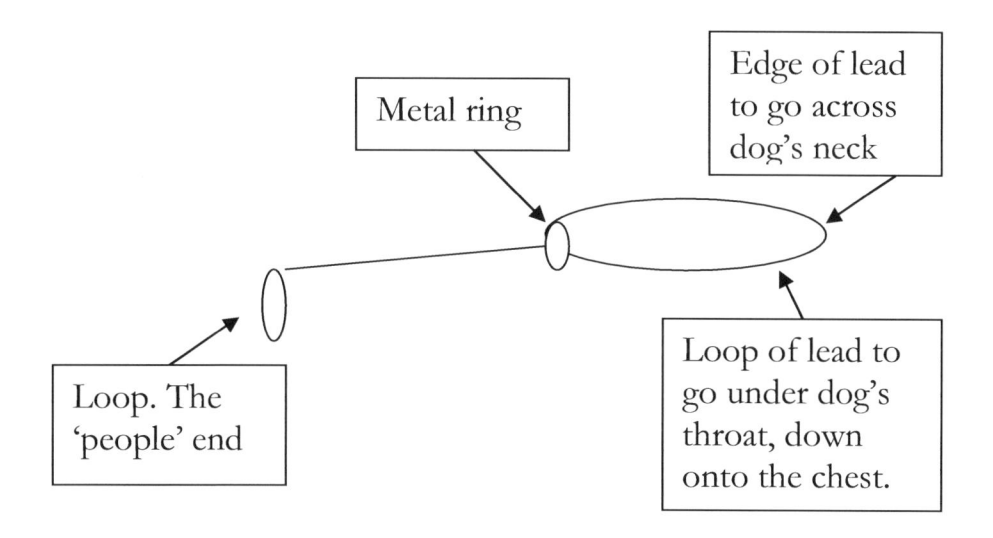

- Metal ring
- Edge of lead to go across dog's neck
- Loop. The 'people' end
- Loop of lead to go under dog's throat, down onto the chest.

The aim is to have a dog stay by your side, off the lead, and to remain in this position no matter what you, the handler, are doing, no matter whether you are walking, standing, sitting, turning corners or turning round, and no matter what may be happening around.

To achieve this eventual goal you need to keep the lead loose more often than it is tight. Anyone, who is big enough and strong enough, can keep a dog on a lead by their side but you need your dog to learn for himself that when you say 'heel' that is where he should be, so always have a loose lead and only let the lead tighten briefly when the dog is out of position. As soon as the dog is in the correct position, there should be no tightness felt by the dog and the leather stop should never be tightened. The reason for this is that a tight lead round the dog's throat is a punishment and as such should be used briefly but effectively so that the dog learns from it rather than just getting used to feeling uncomfortable all the time.

Many people worry when they first decide to put a lead on a young puppy and in fact many people delay this for a considerable time, knowing they will probably have a battle on their hands. Handlers therefore delay or they do things such as put a collar and lead on a puppy and let the puppy run around with the lead on their own – i.e. the handler does not hold onto the lead, or they try and pretend to the puppy that there is no lead on the dog and play with the puppy trying to encourage the puppy to adopt something like the heel position.

These actions, in my opinion, are more to do with a handler not wanting to teach the puppy properly and have more to do with the handlers own sensibilities, than anything to do with wanting to help the puppy learn right from the start, what is required. One day, this will have to be done, so I feel it is much better for a handler to decide 'today I am going to give the puppy a short lesson in heel work', and just go out and do it!

Puppies do not, in general, like being on a lead. They suddenly find their movements and wishes are restricted and controlled, not necessarily by the handler, but by this 'thing round their neck'. This may be the first time a puppy has been confined or controlled in this way.

Handlers need therefore to start heelwork knowing that the dog will not like it. How long the dog dislikes the experience will then depend entirely on the handler. The handler should aim for this experience to be a bit of a shock to the puppy at first but for this to last only a few minutes.

Once a handler has decided that a puppy should have the first lesson on the lead, the handler needs to teach the dog, at the start, exactly what is required. To do this is a simple, but not necessarily an easy task.

A dog is never required to run around and play with a lead on, a dog is never required to follow a handler whilst the handler crawls along the floor or ground playing or pretending that there is no lead around the dog's neck, a dog can never learn exactly what 'heel' means by a handler saying such things as, 'come on, clever puppy, here's a tit-bit, come to me' and hundreds of other words and phrases which I have heard uttered: so I believe we should treat our dogs like the intelligent creatures they most definitely are, and enable them to learn from us, their leaders, exactly what we want of them.

There are dozens of ways in which we can teach a puppy *not* to do what we require, and when it comes to heelwork I believe there to be only one way of teaching a puppy what I require of him now, tomorrow, next week, next year and every day for the rest of his life.

That lesson is learnt at about 10 weeks of age, the lesson lasts at most, for 5 minutes and the lesson is remembered and adhered to for life. As an investment proposition, this is pretty impressive because it means that if you invest 5 minutes you get in return approximately 5,260,000 minutes over the next 10 years. If these minutes were £'s, none of us would hesitate to slap down our £5 notes!

If you want to take this unique opportunity to invest, you get a limited time to sign-up but for those wanting to know more, read on…………..

The reason I teach a puppy at about 10 weeks is that by this time most puppies have had a few weeks either getting used to their new home having come from their breeder home, or getting used to life in the home in which they were bred, but without litter brothers and sisters perhaps. The puppy is eagerly soaking up all the new information in the environment and is at a stage whereby it is curious, wanting to learn and eager to please.

It is also still small enough to pick up and carry!

When the 'today I am going to give the puppy a short lesson in heel work' moment comes, this is what you should do.

The most important aspect is to get yourself in the right frame of mind to be the teacher as well as disciplining yourself to carry on regardless of what the puppy may do to dissuade you from teaching him. Decide where this lesson is going to take place. You do not need acres of ground, so even a small back lawn will suffice or a hallway in the house. Anywhere which is safe and free from too many distractions like other people, dogs, cats, etc. and I prefer not to take the puppy out in the car for this first lesson, so home is best.

Put a slip lead in your pocket, pick up the puppy and carry it to the area where you have decided to work. Slip the lead over the puppy's head, before you put the puppy on the ground. I like to say 'put your lead on' at this point because although the puppy has no idea what it means, he will eventually and it is part of my 'start as you mean to go on' philosophy. When the lead is on the puppy, and you are holding onto the 'people end' your next task will be to put the puppy onto the ground in the correct 'heel' position which is on your left hand side, parallel to your left leg about 6 inches away. There should be no delaying on your part at this point, so your next immediate task is to look down at the puppy and in a normal pleasant voice, and with a smile on your face, say 'heel' and walk.

Your body language is very important and your attitude of mind, which will reflect on your body language, should indicate to the puppy that this is simply another thing, in a long chain of events, which they have to learn and cope with. Unless you can adopt a 'matter of fact' attitude, don't give the lesson! If you need to, practice carrying something into the garden and putting a lead round its 'neck', putting the item on the ground in the correct position, and then just walking! Physically, the actions are simple. It is the mental attitude of a handler, which can make this a difficult procedure for the puppy.

It is your responsibility to walk, no matter what the puppy decides to do. Many puppies, when they realize they are restricted by the lead will cry, may sit down, may lie down, may try to get the lead off, may turn somersaults and may, in fact do absolutely everything and anything, rather than walk by the side of the handler. These are experiments; they are the means by which a puppy learns; they are the equivalent of him saying 'I've got a situation here which I have never experienced before, so how do I cope with it?' The only way a handler can help a puppy with this is to assume an attitude of 'this is no big deal; I'm not worried, so you should not be worried either'.

Now and again a rare puppy just trots along by the handler but don't expect your puppy to do this at the start and then you will be prepared for anything the puppy may do.

Your job is to keep walking but be ready to praise the puppy immediately he is in the correct position walking by your side, with a 'good boy/good girl' in a warm tone of voice. Remember to keep in mind that you are teaching the puppy what is required of him and the only way he can find this out is by experiments of his own, the encouragement he gets from doing and trying to do the right thing and by the praise you give him for appropriate actions.

When he is doing any of the wrong things, i.e. performing any action which you don't want, it is best to ignore them at this stage so just keep walking until you get an opportunity to praise and let the puppy find out for himself that 'oh, I see, when I walk by the leader, the leader is pleased with me, so I think I'll do this forever now!'

Handlers create tremendous problems for a puppy if they stop as soon as a puppy performs any of the experiment actions and many make it even worse by stroking the puppy and praising him. Such handlers say they are trying to reassure a puppy, but there actions seem almost to be apologizing for being so cruel as to put a lead on and far from reassuring or helping the puppy, they are in fact praising the puppy for doing the opposite of what the handler wants. This type of handler behaviour only prolongs the discomfort for the puppy and also gives the impression to the puppy of a weak leader, a leader who cannot be bothered to teach what is required.

If the handler keeps walking, no matter what the puppy is doing, the puppy quickly realizes that if he gets onto his feet and trots along by the side of the handler, the handler will praise him, will look at him and smile, and life is not too bad. It is all over in a matter of seconds or minutes and the puppy has perhaps learnt his first important lesson from the handler, which is when the handler gives a command, it must be obeyed.

For this first lesson, once the puppy is walking appropriately he should be praised and the lesson should then end by the puppy being taken back to the house, kennel or car. Do not just let the puppy off the lead and let him charge around and play. Let him go back to an appropriate place and think about what he has just done. Depending on the puppy, and how the handler approaches this first lesson, it could all be finished in two or three minutes.

If you really feel you are making absolutely no progress with this, and it is getting beyond you to continue after 10 minutes or so, wait until the puppy is in the correct position, praise him, pick him up and carry him into the house and remove the lead. It is important to wait until the puppy is correct, even if it has been short-lived, before giving up. Simply put the puppy on his own, to rest and think. Make yourself a cup of coffee (or something stronger) and you have a think too about why it is taking longer than anticipated. Some time later – at least an hour, go and try again. I promise that it will be better!

Hopefully you will have few problems and the whole first experience will be over within a few minutes. This, to me, is a far kinder way of teaching than an approach which, may seem kinder, but lengthens the time – sometimes over a life-time, when the puppy is uncomfortable with being on a lead because he has not been taught initially of exactly what is required of him.

The next time the handler takes the puppy out, there may be some repetition of inappropriate behaviour when on the lead, but it is usually short-lived, and most puppies simply walk with the handler, because this is the last experience they had.

This does not mean that the puppy now knows what 'heel' means or has learnt to walk to heel appropriately. The handler will need many short sessions of heelwork and these should develop to incorporate turns to the left and right and about turns. This helps the puppy to learn where the heel position is, but also teaches the puppy to watch the handler and position himself in relation to the handler.

It is the responsibility of the handler to ensure that the puppy remains in the correct position and to make sure that when the puppy is in the correct position, that he is given a lot of verbal praise of good boy/good girl so that the puppy begins to understand that 'yes, you are doing the right thing, and I am pleased with you'. It is also vital that if the puppy is in the wrong position, that the handler should correct this immediately with the lead.

To correct an out of position dog the handler will need to give a strong, quick jerk downwards on the lead in the direction of the correct position so, dependant on where the dog is, the jerk will be forward, backward or sideways. Just before the jerk I usually make a growl sound to indicate to the dog that he is doing wrong. The jerk must be quick and the lead allowed to loosen immediately the dog is back in the correct position and as soon as the dog is in position verbal praise, 'good boy/girl' is needed immediately. The growl and the jerk is the way of explaining to the dog that he is in the wrong position and having told him he is wrong, he is then being shown where he needs to put himself to be correct. The verbal praise then says to him 'yes, you are doing the right thing'.

There are various techniques that can be used to help the dog to stay in the correct position; if, by chance, he is in the correct position, he should be praised verbally. In the beginning, if the dog is in the correct position the verbal praise needs almost to be constant whilst dog and handler are walking, this lets the dog know he is being good and doing what is required of him. This enables the dog to relax but also ensures that the dog concentrates on the handler, as he will be looking for the praise.

The first few heelwork sessions should be hard work for the handler, who needs to concentrate on every step taken and be ready, instantly to either correct or praise - both are very important.

Combined with growls, jerks and praise, changing direction is a useful tool so for dogs that pull ahead do a sudden about turn without warning the dog. For dogs that lag behind; quickening the pace to a run if necessary may speed them up or often lagging has been created by a handler constantly towing a dog into the heel position instead of giving a quick jerk on the lead and encouraging the dog to put himself in the correct position. For dogs that pull to the side, walking close up to a wall or hedge or making a sudden 90degree turn to the right may help and also making sure that the correction on the lead has not developed into a gentle towing of the dog into position. 'Towing' i.e. gently pulling the dog along from wherever the dog decides to walk is ineffective as a teaching tool and it looks like a horse on a tow-path, towing a barge on a canal! All the dog learns is that whatever position he is in is appropriate, and he is correct to walk in that position because the handler allows it and in fact encourages it. He gets used to being fairly uncomfortable on the lead, will often look a bit miserable and it is a long way from the vision of a happy puppy trotting by your side, wanting to be with you.

The word 'heel' does not have to be said constantly whilst a handler is walking. The command word should be used when the handler starts walking and when the dog is in the correct position verbal praise should be all that is needed. The 'heel' command should be used again after the dog has been corrected or after a halt and then the handler can continue with the verbal praise again.

CHAPTER FOUR

The 'sit' command

The purpose of teaching a dog what a 'sit' command means is all part of steadiness training as well as being able to command a dog to adopt a position whereby the dog can relax and switch off slightly because the dog eventually learns that he will not be required to do anything or go anywhere until he is given another command.

All dogs know how to sit from when they are 2 weeks old so we do not need to teach a dog to sit but we need to teach it to adopt that position when we give the command word. The purpose therefore, unlike teaching a 'heel' command, which is to teach a dog our meaning of the word, is that for a 'sit' we need to teach a dog what to do when he hears the command 'sit'.

The sit position for a gundog is not quite the same as taught for some dog disciplines in that for gundogs usually, it is not vital that the dog sits straight for example as it would have to do in competition obedience. It is not strictly necessary for a gundog to sit in any circumstances but most people teach a sit for the reasons given above in terms of steadiness and relaxing. Other than this there is no specific requirement for a dog to sit at heel when walking up, sit to present a bird or dummy or to sit on recall but all these aspects are felt by many handlers to be important in terms of gaining control of a dog in the early stages of training. Later on, many people do not command or expect a dog to sit when for example, walking up or to present a bird and are quite happy for the dog to do these things from and in a stand position.

Training

To begin teaching the 'sit' position you need to decide which command you are going to use i.e. which word you are going to attach to a specific action or position for your dog.

I use the word 'sit'. You must decide for yourself, which word you will use (some people use 'hup', which is a contraction of the words 'sit up', or 'drop') but I will use the word 'sit' throughout.

The definition of the sit command to the dog is: 'put your bottom on the ground and have your chest off the ground.'

The teaching method used is one of positioning and praise.

The sit command is best taught in conjunction with heelwork on the lead and in that way it can be ensured that the handler has some control over the dog. Remember that the requirement is to teach the dog what the handler means, and therefore what the dog should do, when given the command word 'sit'. There is no point therefore in a handler saying the word and then doing nothing to help the dog understand what is required.

For the definition of the command, the dog needs to be taught an action or position. The command word does not mean a location, so the place in which the dog sits needs to be determined by the timing of when the handler gives the command. For example: if the handler is walking with the dog and the dog is required to sit in the heel position (remember the definition of the heel position), the handler will need to ensure that the dog is in the heel position before giving the 'sit' command.

The dog needs to be taught too that he must obey commands immediately, so if the dog is given a 'sit' command when he is in the wrong location the result will be a dog sitting with his back to the handler, sitting 2 yards in front or sitting too far behind. Timing is therefore an important part of the exercise and handlers need to be aware of all the implications when they start.

When first practicing heelwork, handlers should have a few short sessions of that alone first so that the dog is beginning to understand the heel position. The handler can then start teaching a 'sit' command without too many other problems.

To begin, do some heelwork on the lead, check and ensure that your dog is in the correct heel position and then stop walking. As you are in the process of stopping give the command 'sit' in a normal, pleasant voice, and immediately bend down and place the dog in the sit position and say 'good boy/girl' as soon as the dog is in position. You are saying the word, showing the dog what the word means and praising verbally.

Some handlers have difficulty in positioning the dog in this way.

The way I do it is this:

- Think first about what is to happen.
- Stop walking and at the same time say the command word 'sit'.
- The right hand (which is holding the lead) should drop downwards and whilst still holding the lead with the right hand, place the right hand onto the dog's chest, and apply slight pressure backwards. At the same time, the left hand should be placed on the dog's lower back, just where the tail joins onto the body, and slight pressure downwards applied. It is a rocking movement rather than one of pushing.
- The movements by the handler should be swift and the right hand on the chest should exert more pressure in a backward direction than the left hand on the rump in a downward direction, although both hands work together.
- As soon as the dog is in position the hands should be removed whilst the handler says 'good boy/girl' and stands up straight.

Don't assume that your dog now knows what to do when you say 'sit'. For several sessions always place the dog in position. You will need to do the same things all the time and if you do this, you will find one day that your dog will be sitting before you have time to bend down. You will need to test this out however and do a bit more heelwork with some turns and quick stops with 'sit' commands. If your dog does not sit immediately you give the command, go back to placing him. Do not get cross; getting cross with the dog will not enable him to learn any quicker and getting cross will prevent the handler teaching, so stay calm and go on teaching for a few more sessions.

Remember to praise your dog verbally every time he obeys a command, even if you have put him in position. This way the dog learns what you want of him and life becomes simple for him – he learns to obey and is praised when he is right!

If you want a dog to obey all your commands instantly you need to discipline yourself very carefully. Be consistent, and make sure you always give the correct command for the position you expect your dog to be in. If you are doing heel work, stop and give a 'sit' command make sure, when you set off walking again, that you then give a 'heel' command and praise the dog.

Later on in the training programme, you will be giving a 'sit' command and then walking away without the dog, so now is the time to show your dog that you expect him to go on obeying a command, once given, until you give another command. You need also to be teaching yourself that this is precisely what you will do.

If these exact steps are taken, nothing can go wrong!

Invariably, however, things do go wrong and almost always this is because a handler is not following the precise routine. If anything appears to be going wrong it is best to stop and consider everything and if needed, get someone to watch you and the dog. Few of us are aware of the things we are doing all the time. For new handlers the most frequent problems occur due to one of the following reasons:

The handler has:

- Stopped teaching the dog by positioning and praise
- Started giving more than one command
- Started shouting the command word
- Failed to praise the dog immediately he is correct
- Tried to stop the dog by pulling up on the lead
- Begun to hold the lead too high on stopping so that the dog cannot sit without the danger of strangling himself.

Some handlers give up teaching their dog too early before the dog has fully understood, not only what he has to do but that he must do it instantly he hears the command. Handlers who cannot be bothered to go on teaching the dog in precisely the same way will frequently get out of teaching mode and into either a punishing mode, or get into the habit of giving more than one command to the dog. This is not what we want and the longer a handler can persevere with teaching by positioning and praising the more likely-hood there is of the dog learning exactly what to do which is sit; when to do it which is now; and to do it quickly on the one and only command given so that he is given praise immediately.

For novice handlers their greatest problem is that they stop teaching too early. It is difficult to give a precise time scale for this but it is wise to err on the side of caution and go on for many weeks with positioning and praise and never command a dog to sit at any other time than when doing heelwork on the lead. Many handlers start too early to give a sit command to their dog in other circumstances such as in the house, when the handler has no lead on the dog and may not be close to the dog. This then gives the dog the opportunity to disobey the command when the handler is not in a position to enforce it so, however tempting it may be to test whether the dog will sit, it is much better not to give the command in any circumstances, at this stage, other than when in the process of a short training session with the lead.

Apart from teaching for too short a time, many handlers also find it difficult, for some reason, to praise a dog verbally. I have never been able to understand why it is so difficult for some people to say 'good boy' in a warm and friendly voice. Many people will insist on praising with their hands so that they are constantly stroking and petting the dog as a substitute, the handlers think, for praising the dog. There are a few reasons why this type of physical contact praise is not desirable from a training point of view;

- For a partnership between gundog and handler to work satisfactorily, a handler needs eventually to be able to send their dog away from them and for the dog to work at a distance, sometimes for a considerable time and sometimes having to obey numerous commands. If a dog has to be helped to locate a wounded bird for example, a handler may have to give several directional commands to the dog. When the dog obeys these, the voice is all a handler has to utilize when they need to praise and encourage the dog. A handler does not want a dog returning too quickly or not continuing to work. I said earlier that I train a dog from the beginning in the way I expect for life and it is important for a dog to learn early in life that verbal praise will be his reward and he therefore will gain confidence at working further away from the handler and be confident to remain working at a distance because he can be rewarded and praised at a distance.
- Some handlers do not realize how much they put their hands onto a dog. In the majority of cases, it is the handler who needs reassurance from the dog and they gain security from the frequent physical contact. This gives all the wrong messages to the dog, who requires the handler to be a strong leader. A leader who needs their confidence boosted by the troops continually will soon loose respect from them! The dog is not in a position to reassure a handler at this level, it is not the dog's responsibility to reassure the

handler and eventually it could give the dog a false sense of superiority. A handler, from the dog's point of view, should be confident, all knowing and capable of dealing with whatever life throws at the partnership.

🐾 When handlers use physical, often continual, gentle stroking, particularly when the handler does not realize they are doing it, the handler will be giving a message of approval to the dog. The chances are that at least 50% of these messages will be inappropriate in that whatever the dog happens to be doing will be rewarded by stroking. The dog is therefore being taught, and therefore learning (a) when he is correct, the praise he will be given to encourage more of the correct behaviour, is being stroked. AND (b) When he is incorrect he will also be rewarded by being stroked. It does not take a genius to realize that: if we were all given our wages at our work place for (a) arriving on time each day and working to the best of our ability AND (b) not turning up at all or turning up and not working, which option we would all go for!

Teaching a dog to sit on command requires very little of a handler. It is such a simple procedure to say 'Sit', bend down, position the dog, stand up straight, look at the dog, smile and say 'good boy' in a warm and pleasant voice. All a handler has to do is teach. All a dog can do is learn, correctly, what is being taught. It is not hard for the dog. It should not be hard for the handler either.

Use of the word 'Stay'.

I never use the word 'stay' in training.

I have never been able to work out how to teach a dog effectively what the word means and I have learned by experience that there is more initial unsteadiness in dogs whose handlers have tried to teach 'stay' than in dogs whose handlers have not tried to teach the word. I accept that eventually dogs will learn to remain in position in one place but only usually by being punished and I believe the whole concept of 'stay' is a difficult one for a dog to grasp quickly or easily.

Let us examine exactly what happens in a so called 'stay'. A handler commands the dog to adopt a certain, taught and learned position of 'sit', 'down' or 'stand'. The handler gives the command; the dog obeys and adopts the required position. The handler's intention is then, to leave the dog, walk away from the dog, and the dog is required to maintain the position and remain in the same spot i.e. stay there in that particular position. The handler, before walking away therefore says or shouts 'stay' and walks away.

From a dog's point of view this must be very difficult and I have seen time after time, dogs which then follow their handler. This in turn leads to handlers shouting at the dog and often man-handling it back to the spot he should have 'stayed'. The handler has no way of explaining in words to the dog what 'stay' means, has no method of teaching the dog what 'stay' means other than in fact setting the dog up to fail and then punishing the dog. Eventually the dog learns what 'stay' means, but what a performance! How unjust!

Apart from having to learn through experimentation and punishment it is unjust for the following reason. If a handler teaches a dog what to do on the command 'sit' the dog will have learned that following his instant obedience he will be rewarded in some way. The day a handler decides to start on 'stay' training however, the dog will start by obeying the 'sit' command and then, instead of his expected reward, the handler will shout 'stay'. Now a dog, as any intelligent creature would on being shouted at, should immediately believe he is doing something wrong. As the only thing he is doing at that time is sitting, he would also immediately think 'oh dear, I've got it wrong and I should not be sitting at all'. The dog has therefore only one option. He does not know what 'stay' means and as it obviously does not mean 'sit', because it sounds different, he will get up and try to guess what this new sound 'stay' means. Whatever he does at this stage will involve him in punishment from the handler because he will never, no matter what he decides to do, get it right.

My preferred method is to teach a dog the positions they should adopt in relation to command words of 'sit', 'down' or 'stand' or whatever positions are needed. In so doing, I will also be teaching a dog that 'you go on doing that, maintaining that position, until I tell you to do something else. You keep to that position no matter what I am doing, no matter what other people and other dogs are doing, and no matter what is going on around you'.

It is true that I cannot explain this in words to the dog, as he has to learn this over time but, I believe that if I have to punish a dog in any way, I should punish a dog for disobeying me on something I know I have taught and I know he has learned. For example: I teach a dog what he should do when I say 'sit'. If I then walk away from the dog and the dog moves, I can legitimately apply some kind of punishment because the dog has disobeyed my 'sit' command. This needs to be built up gradually in stages however and later on it will be shown how this is achieved in training.

(e) Young puppies and 'holding'.

A puppy 7 weeks of age picking up and carrying a tennis ball which she found in the garden.

The ball was not thrown for the puppy but she is encouraged to share and happy to 'give'.

CHAPTER FIVE

Hold and Give commands

Most retrievers, and other gundogs which have retrieving as part of their role, have no problem in holding something in their mouth. They have known how to hold something and carry it around since they were a few weeks old and it was probably one of the first things they learned to do for themselves, through play, when growing up with their breeder, dam and litter brothers and sisters. Puppies will also have learned how to take possession of items which they want and, depending on their temperament and their position in the hierarchy, will have learned how to defend and relinquish possessions.

It is important when a puppy joins his new domestic pack that he learns that he cannot have everything he wants and even if he is allowed to have certain things that every human from a toddler upwards is in a higher position than he and as such *owns* everything. We need therefore to begin to show a puppy that when he has something in his mouth, his job is to bring it to his handler and when he does this he will be handsomely rewarded with praise. We also need to teach him that he will never be scolded or punished in any way when he has something in his mouth. This is the first step towards having a gundog whose chief function, when he is an adult, trained dog will be to retrieve shot, dead and wounded birds and bring them straight back to his handler.

We also need to put a command word onto the act of 'holding' something and teach a puppy that having something in his mouth and carrying it is called 'hold', or whatever word you choose to mean hold. In conjunction with this, and arguably of more importance, a dog has to learn to release anything in his mouth when a human takes hold of the item and gives him the command word to relinquish it. This word will be his command to give the item to the human. I use 'give' for this, many people use the word 'dead' and it does not matter which word you choose but I shall use the word 'give' throughout.

Some people use the word 'drop' but I believe it is not a particularly good word, in that it has connotations of doing just that – releasing the item and dropping it on the ground. A gundog should always hold onto any item until the handler also has hold of it. The item should never be dropped and although the dog does not understand what 'drop' means, many handlers can inadvertently teach a dog to drop something simply because that is the idea the human has in his own mind, connected with the word.

The reason gundogs should never actually drop anything, is that one of their important roles on a shoot is to retrieve wounded birds which are sometimes called 'runners'. Depending on where on the body the bird has been injured, many wounded birds, when they fall to the ground, do just that – run, often very quickly. If a dog has to go after one of these runners, successfully retrieves it and brings it to the handler, the last thing we need is for the dog to drop the wounded bird. Most birds would take the opportunity to run off again, and this time, the dog may not be so successful in retrieving it. It is also important not to use the word 'drop' for a hold command, if you have used this word to mean 'sit' or any other position.

Probably the best way of beginning the process of teaching the 'hold' and 'give' commands is in the house and not as part of a more formal training session. You need to teach the words 'hold' and 'give' at the same time.

Presenting.

Presenting a dummy, toy, shot bird or any item to a handler, is the term used to mean the final part of a retrieve. It is the moment when your dog is sitting in front of you with his head up, the item in his mouth, waiting for you to take hold of the item, give the release command, the dog releasing the item and remaining in the sit position in front of you whilst waiting for his next command.

It is important to build the 'sit in front, *after* releasing the item', into the training regime, because it is at this point that the handler will be dealing with the item presented, which has nothing to do with the dog. This means the handler is either putting a dummy, into their bag, or possibly dispatching a wounded bird or placing a dead bird in a game carrier.

In order for the handler to concentrate on these tasks it is essential that the dog is steady, not pestering, not jumping up trying to grab back the item just released and in general is behaving himself. The last thing a handler needs at this stage is for their dog to believe 'OK I've done that, I'm going off to have some fun on my own' and in order for this *not* to happen, handlers must build this aspect into the training at an early stage and create routines which will be required for life.

Some dogs appear to have a fairly natural 'present' and are eager to show that they have retrieved just for you, and are then presenting the item almost 'gift wrapped'! Other dogs, give the impression that they have retrieved for themselves and although happy to return to you, they are not going to release the item or they squirm around and do everything they can to make it difficult for you to take the item from them or they spit it out too quickly or almost throw it at the handler and immediately take off at speed to see if they can find something else. Worst of all are the dogs which work entirely for themselves and although going out for a retrieve, really have no intention of bringing it anywhere near their handler and in fact go off in the opposite direction.

I believe that handlers actually create a 'present', good or bad, and the time they create it is well before, or during the basic training and this should be a long time before any actual retrieving is done.

Many handlers set the scene for poor presenting, without realizing that they are doing so, and by the time they realize they have a problem, the problem is often difficult to correct. I have said before, that the solution to any problem never lies at the point where you see the problem, but lies much further back in the training. With the present the solution may lie in a number of different areas and it may not be possible to undo some problems, as you cannot revisit the scenes where they were created.

The start of poor presenting, and other retrieving problems, could begin as early as 7/8 weeks of age, but often it begins when you first react, to something you see that a puppy has in his mouth. The human reaction only springs into action when a pup is first seen to have something which the human values at that particular time i.e. he is running round the garden with your one and only pair of decent tights or socks, has a child's homework/book/game, has someone's wallet and is extracting cheque book, money and credit cards.

The human reaction therefore is one of horror, and usually involves feverish activity of running, gesticulating and shouting until the puppy is cornered, grabbed, shouted at, mouth opened, article extracted and then more shouting. You get the picture! Prior to this big traumatic event, anything the puppy was holding, which was unimportant to humans was probably ignored and no-one has taken much notice of what the puppy was carrying or in fact what he was doing with it.

Neither of these actions by humans is appropriate, or helpful, in teaching a puppy what he should do when he finds something and is holding it, although the latter is probably preferable of the two, provided it is the reaction continually.

If a puppy is chased or is shouted at, it is teaching the puppy that sometimes when he has something in his mouth life becomes rather unpleasant and even though he may enjoy the experience of having something in his mouth, he certainly will not share the experience with any human that happens to be around. It also teaches the puppy that whenever he has something in his mouth, his best bet is to run off with the item and not show himself until he has eaten or torn the item into little bits. The fact that one or more humans chase him and shout when he has something in his mouth, will give the puppy the information that he is leader of the pack – they were all following him making a noise of excitement and joining in the chase.

This is not the message a puppy should be getting.

The 1st prevention rule must be to try and keep all items of value out of reach of a puppy. Training therefore should start with the whole family putting their prize possessions out of harms way. This should be part of your preparation before the puppy comes home to your domestic pack, when you are making sure that electric cables are barricaded in, ornaments taken from low tables and there are no dangers to the puppy from items around the home and there are no dangers to items around the home from the puppy. Inevitably you will not have thought of everything, or everyone starts to be less vigilant and things start to be left around so there will come the day when the puppy has something you would rather he did not have. When this happens, you need to train yourself to react in the fashion of; 'what a clever puppy to find something which one of us humans has inadvertently left around'. You may have to act this bit but it is important! This way your puppy will see an expression of pleasure, admiration, approval and love on your face.

He will probably have learnt already that this expression means that everything in life is fine, so act the feeling, paint on the expression and just crouch down. Usually a pup will come dashing over to see you, carrying the item and you can praise him, 'good boy' and then just chat, 'you are a clever boy, what have you got'? It does not matter what you say but just keep it happy and cheerful - pups like soppy talk! The important thing to remember at this point is to go on chatting and praising – *you are praising him for coming to you and for having something in his mouth*. There is absolutely no way I can think of, to say 'yes you are doing the right thing for coming to me'; 'yes you are doing the right thing for retrieving'; but 'no, you are doing the wrong thing by having that *particular item* in your mouth'.

The praise will hopefully keep him with you. Do not attempt to grab the puppy or the item. Keep on praising and stroking the puppy and while he is squirming around, mentally plot your next move!

Your next move is to try and get hold of part of the item which is in his mouth, with one hand, and open his mouth with your other hand, whilst continuing to tell him what a very clever boy he is.

When you have hands in position put in the word 'give' and then you can take the item and then praise the pup again. You should immediately then give the puppy something he can have.

Training

By far the best method is to be proactive in training on these matters, rather than waiting until the above situation where you have to be reactive. Teach a puppy, through play first and by encouraging a puppy to come to you. You do not need to do anything, other than get down on the floor with a young puppy and he will want to be there with you. If he has some toys around he will be happy to share these with you and if you see the puppy with something in his mouth encourage him to share it. If you show yourself willing to participate in some play when the puppy has something he is *allowed* to have such as a dog toy, rather than when he has something of value of yours, you will not have to act, quite as much, in terms of the pleasure you are feeling and conveying to the puppy.

If you start early you will find a puppy bringing everything to you at a very early age. It has its' drawbacks of course when he brings the dead rat or the mouthful of sheep droppings but it is a small price to pay in exchange for a dog who wants to share his retrieves willingly with you and who eventually will retrieve just for you.

It may seem like a lot of hard work but it really isn't! I have had pups as early as 9/10 weeks old, wanting to bring things to me and by the time they are 12 weeks old, sitting in front and presenting properly.

If you constantly encourage a pup to come to you with an item in his mouth, praise him and scratch him on the chest between his front legs, you will find with a little help, he will start to sit in front of you and hold his head up for you to scratch his chest. Sitting in front of you with head up and item in mouth, is what we want for an ideal 'present'.

When you see your dog with something in his mouth start saying the word 'hold' to him, most young puppies are only too eager to come and show you. If the dog does not come to you, don't speak any more, just ignore the dog and try again next time you see he has something in his mouth. Do not try to *make* the dog come to you and do not chase after the dog.

Crouching down on the floor will usually be irresistible to a puppy, so sit on the floor, clap your hands or be very busy with something just out of sight of the puppy and see if the dog comes to you. If he comes to you, keep repeating the word 'hold' while you praise him for a while. Do not grab the puppy or try and take the item from him, but just let him enjoy showing you and if you are able to, scratch his chest in between his front legs.

Then, take hold of the item and say 'give'. It is important at this point to make sure you do not let go of the item. If your dog releases the item immediately, praise him and make a big fuss of him. If he does not release the item, simply open his mouth gently and take the item from him and then praise him. You must not get into a *tug-of-war* situation and if the puppy shows any sign of resistance, simply lift him up and hold him in position, not harshly but just so he cannot believe he is stronger or that it is a game. Releasing an item once a human has hold of it and gives the release command, is not a game but one of those 'must do' situations.

If the item is something which he is allowed to have, just give it back to him without any command word. If the item is something he should not have, put it away and immediately give the puppy something he is allowed to have.

This early play is best at around 8 to 12 weeks, usually before more formal training starts. It is important at this early stage never to throw any toys or anything for a puppy and you will need to ensure that everyone in the household understands this rule. Above all else however, you need to remember that a puppy is never in the wrong when he has something in his mouth. He should never be scolded and always praised. If the puppy has something you feel he should not have, it is not the fault of the puppy. The fault lies with whoever left the object where the puppy could get it or find it! That person is the one who should be scolded therefore, but of course this must be after the puppy has been praised for finding it!

Once a dog is bringing and releasing items of his own choosing quickly on command, you will know then that it is the time to start expecting him to hold items of your choosing. I like to think of this stage of training as being *my* game. It is my game with my toys and my rules and if the puppy is very lucky, he gets to play this game once, every so often, with me.

Start with something soft like an old sock tied with a knot in the middle or a cloth which you can tie into a knot or anything you like which is not too big for the dog to hold but is big enough to hang out of his mouth so you can get hold of it. It should be an item which is not one of his toys and not something he has ever played with or been allowed to hold before. Hold the item in front of the dog and say 'hold' and at the same time open his mouth gently and slip the item into his mouth making sure that his lip is not caught between his teeth and the hold item, which may cause him pain and will discourage him. It is important not to give the dog any choice at this stage so there is no point in simply holding the item in front of the dog and saying 'hold'. If the dog decides he does not want to 'hold' all you would be doing is teaching him *not* to hold when you give him the command.

When the item is in his mouth, you need to praise the dog continually and most puppies will love holding your toy and will enjoy being praised for doing something they like doing. Don't be in a rush to get the item off the dog. You have told him to hold it, he has obeyed and you get an opportunity to go on praising him. Let him savour the experience and it will serve you well in the future.

When you are ready, take hold of the item and say 'give'. He should release it immediately on one command but if he doesn't, do not let go of the item but open his mouth to release the item and then praise him. Just do this once on the first occasion and then make a big show of putting the toy away in a place the puppy cannot get to it. I often say 'gone away' at this stage. This 'gone away' is not a command, but an information phrase which will actually come in handy later on.

Repeat the exercise a few times over the following days and do it with different items until he has really understood both commands. Do not overdo this however. Make the occasion special. Doing it once or twice, every so often, appears to work best with this exercise as the puppy sees it as a special thing he is allowed to do with you. Like all special things, they are best experienced infrequently otherwise they become less than special.

When you believe your dog understands what 'hold' means, test this by holding the item in front of the dog and say 'hold'. If your dog has understood the command, he will reach forward and take the item in his mouth. Praise him and let him hold onto it before giving the 'give' command. You will then know that the dog understands what 'hold' means and you can then continue with the exercise in this form, now and again until you have made some progress with more formal training sessions.

The lessons for the handler are:

Do not be tempted to throw anything for your puppy. Try to ensure no-one else throws anything for your puppy. Never scold a puppy when he has something in his mouth. Always praise him when he has something in his mouth and encourage him to share it with you.

Taking Control — 55 —

🐾 **(f) Working with other handlers and dogs to learn various aspects of steadiness.**

Dogs learning to remain in the sit position, no matter what is going on around them. In this case it is another handler and dog, passing by and stopping to speak to all the stationary handlers.

(Below) A handler walking past stationary dogs

(g)

Further developments can include other handlers stopping and stroking a stationary dog, provided both dogs remain at heel in the sit position

CHAPTER SIX

Developing work on heelwork and sits.

Once you have had a few sessions of teaching a dog heelwork on the lead, and introduced teaching the 'sit' command it will be time to give your dog some experience of what all this means in different circumstances.

It is at this stage that it is a good idea to join a puppy or beginner gundog training class. For those training on their own however it is also a time to consider joining up with at least one other person and dog so that your dog can get used to obeying you and doing all the things he has learnt when there is also the distraction of another dog and person or you are in a different location.

It is also good for a handler too in that many handlers feel shy, apprehensive and anxious about working their dog amongst others – 'they go to pieces'! Feelings like this transfer very quickly to the dog and dogs therefore start to have similar feelings. When a dog becomes anxious because it has picked up that their handler, their leader, is worried, it has an adverse affect on training.

It is important therefore for handlers to put themselves into these situations, learn to work with others around, and cope so that they convey the correct leadership qualities to their dogs. Most gundog handlers have to work with others and it is important that this be tackled in training at an early stage so that a handler can learn coping strategies, thus to be able to handle their dog adequately without becoming a quivering wreck every time someone else is present.

If most of your early training sessions have been in your garden, or some secluded spot with no distractions, the time has come to teach the dog that 'heel' means heel *no matter what else is going on around* and that 'sit' means sit *no matter what else is going on around* as well as teaching that 'heel' and 'sit' commands apply *wherever we are and whenever I, the handler, give the command.*

This may appear an easy concept to understand for a person, but to dogs, this has to be learnt in the same way, as they had to learn what position they have to adopt when they hear the words 'heel' or 'sit'. The only way for a dog to learn these things is for a handler to give the dog the experience so he can learn.

Training therefore needs to step up a level and although the dog will not be taught or be learning a new training concept in terms of a new position or a new command word, he needs to be able to learn that the commands he knows already apply here, there and absolutely everywhere. That is: the circumstances may change, there may be other people around, there may be other dogs doing things, you may be working on grass, in woodland or on a stubble field but, when the handler says 'heel' or 'sit' those commands must be obeyed in each and every place they are said, come what may, and no matter what else is different. We need to teach the dog that *Commands will never change, but circumstances will change.*

When you first go to a new place or your dog is experiencing new people or other dogs there is no point in trying to start at the point you had reached with the dog in the seclusion of your own garden. So, you should aim to start at a point below the standard already achieved. If you join a training class you will probably be doing quite a lot of heelwork and sits on the lead in the company of several other people and dogs and you and your dog may well have to wait for your turn to do something whilst someone else is working. This is all valuable experience for you and your dog and an important opportunity for you to reinforce the parts of training your dog may already have learnt.

If the standard you have reached appears a little higher than others in the class, do not feel that the class is a waste of time for you because you will have the opportunity of seeing for yourself whether:

what you have taught your dog so far, has been learned by the dog; whether he can sit in the heel position on a loose lead whilst other dogs are walking past him; whether he will remain in that position when he sees a dog at a distance doing something he would like to do; whether he can resist jumping up or trying to run off and play with another dog. These are all vital experiences for handler and dog but the dog will only gain some advantage from this if the handler is concentrating.

So often in a class situation handlers will work when it is their turn, but when it is the turn of someone else the handler will switch off. Instead of using the time effectively by insisting that the dog continues to behave correctly a handler will for example, say 'heel' and then allow the dog to be anywhere *but* the heel position; will say 'sit' and then start talking to the neighbouring handler and cease to be aware that their dog is in fact lying down or trying to play with the dog on the other side. Sometimes handlers are aware of what their dog may be doing, but if the dog is not pestering them they tend to ignore the fact that the dog is disobeying, which is not what should happen when you are teaching a dog how to obey. All this does, is teach a dog how *not* to obey and this is a dangerous path to tread.

You do not want your dog to believe that he only obeys at certain times. He needs to believe that he must obey each and every command you give, every time, on the first time of asking; otherwise you will develop a *performing* dog rather than an obedient dog. If you pay attention to your own dog even when you are waiting for your turn you can also act as a useful role model to others in the class who may not have reached your standard, and will be trying to pick up tips on how to achieve the standards required.

If you feel your standard is lower than others in the class, it is important also not to feel the class is a waste of your time. There will inevitably be differences in the skills and expertise of the handlers in any group, particularly if the group has been formed based on the age or standard of the dogs. You should never feel you are wasting other people's time or worry that you are holding others back due to any problems you may be having.

A good instructor will make sure that everyone is helped in some way during the course of the lesson and everyone will need some help at some point. It may be you who appears to be in need of the most help on one session, but you can almost guarantee that it will be someone else in need of this on the next and subsequent lessons. No one person and no dog is the same as any other, in terms of their learning abilities and skills, on each and every concept to be learned. So, instead of worrying, use the opportunities given to you, and try to do what an instructor is telling and showing you. If you are not certain what an instructor means, ask and watch others in the class when they are doing things being taught. They may not be doing exactly the same as you are working on with your dog, but it is information which you may need at some point.

Widening a dog's experience and knowledge is not about trying to teach the dog as many commands as you can, but ensuring that each and every command you teach the dog will be obeyed under all circumstances. Teaching should therefore be concerned with doing the same things in as many different places as possible and trying to incorporate sensible and incremental distractions to reinforce the dog's learning in positive ways.

In a training group situation many techniques will be used to help all the handlers and dogs learn. Heelwork may be done in a circle with everyone walking round at the same time, or in a straight line with everyone walking together and keeping the line straight. It may be practised with most of the group standing still with one handler and dog weaving their way in and out of the stationary handlers and dogs or with half the group walking in the opposite direction so that each handler and dog passes several others in the course of walking. Sometimes several or all the handlers and dogs will be working at the same time, sometimes each handler and dog will work on their own. All these techniques will help dogs to learn that they should ignore everything but their own handler and this should mean to the dog that, yes they can watch what is going on, but they cannot join in if they have been commanded to sit or heel.

These lessons are much better learnt when dogs are young. Dogs that may have spent a year or more pleasing themselves, ignoring their handler, and going off to play and investigate anything exciting whenever it suits them, will take much longer to learn these new rules, and some, unfortunately, will never learn them because they will not be taught!

Puppies should therefore, in my opinion, never be allowed too much free play or freedom to do as they like other than in very limited circumstances such as in a small area of garden when they can play and do what they like for limited periods of time on their own or in the company of another trusted and trained dog with whom they live. Puppies should not be taken out and then let off the lead. They do not need it and owners wishing to train their dogs in a constructive manner will find if they give this type of freedom to the dog, many dogs will be much harder to train and some may be impossible to train.

This type of behaviour by an owner is also, in my opinion, irresponsible. To let a dog off the lead other than in ones own garden, before one has the means, through training: to stop the dog going anywhere he may be in danger, for example running onto a road; or to command the dog to return to you immediately; is putting not only the dog at risk but may be putting other people, other dogs or livestock at risk too. The majority of people would not let a young child walk by themselves in any circumstances where the child may be at risk, yet they put at risk a young puppy by allowing it inappropriate freedom. Some adult humans take more care over a recently purchased £5 bottle of wine than a puppy costing many hundreds of pounds and it never ceases to amaze me!

Yes, dogs need some exercise, but they do not need as much physical exercise as many people believe. If you train a puppy for 5 minutes he will be tired at the end of it because he has had to use his brain as well as his muscles and 5 minutes training has a great deal more value than one hour free running. Two or three 5 minute training sessions throughout the day with one or two 'free time' short play sessions in a garden or confined space is sufficient, and if you have to miss a home training session it is never a good idea to try and make it up by doing a longer time on the next opportunity.

I believe that a puppy should get his greatest enjoyment from being allowed to work with me, his leader, and anything a puppy does with me, as his leader in the first few months is work: the puppy is *on duty*, learning how to be part of my pack, which he will view as a privilege. I therefore do not allow puppies to do anything which they will not be allowed to do later in life, and I train a puppy right from the start that everything I teach him will be used throughout life in exactly the same way.

In developing the experience for a dog by using different types of training area and by ensuring that a dog understands that commands must be obeyed 'no matter what', it is also important to begin building in some other changes. If you always do the same things in the same order a dog may learn that some commands may only apply when preceded or followed by others, so it is important to vary things to some degree. Obviously at the start of training you will have taught very little, and the dog will not be able to do a great deal. However, even in the early stages it is vital that, for example, you don't always follow a pattern of heelwork in a straight line; turns to the left, then turns to the right; then about turns; so vary the order in which you practice exercises.

Training sessions should involve keeping the attention of the dog and making sure you are entirely predictable on some things, and this means on commands, but are entirely unpredictable in terms of how and where you do your training sessions, the order in which you practice various exercises and the circumstances when you will give a command. If you are in a training group, or even with just one other handler and dog, make sure the order you work on individual exercises changes too. One dog should never get the idea of 'I am always first' or even 'I'm always last'.

It is also important, I believe, for a puppy or older dog to have some time after the training session, to be on his own to 'think'. I know some people will not believe in this concept but I firmly believe that a training session, followed by a period alone either in the back of the car, in a cage in the house, in a kennel, or just left alone in the kitchen on his bed, more than doubles the benefit of however long the training session lasted. The time out to think may not always be possible, but if this can be built into your training regime, the benefits should become obvious very quickly. Whether a period of isolation in this way is possible or not, it is never, in my opinion, appropriate to allow the dog to simply go off and play and possibly risk undoing any progress or learning achieved in your training session. Five minutes training followed immediately by ten minutes isolation and rest totals nearly one hour of learning and it is the ten minutes rest which achieves the most benefit provided the five minutes training has been appropriate, constructive, and correct. Remember also that if the five minutes training has been inappropriate, incorrect and less than constructive, that the dog will use the rest period to learn about the benefits of that too! These benefits will be less than desirable as far as the handler is concerned and will be destructive to the whole training purpose rather than of benefit!

Handlers too should take the opportunity to think before and after a training session. If you are working on your own the thinking beforehand should involve planning what you intend to do. After the session you need to think about what was achieved, what went wrong, how you plan to further the learning or change things next time and examine your role as a teacher to your dog? Notes can then be made in preparation for the next session.

If you have been to a training class it is a good idea to write down what you did, how you personally benefited or where it went wrong for you. If you have not understood something and were not able to ask, make a note to ask or discuss the concept with the instructor and if you are not sure about something do not try and teach your dog.

In a class situation, you will often be shown something which you then go and practice at home in readiness for the next training session. It is often vital to teach dogs things in the correct order so that each new aspect of training is carefully added at the right time. For novice handlers therefore it is preferable not to try and teach your dog anything until you have been shown how to teach it. This will then ensure that you and your dog will be given the best possible chance of getting each new concept correct rather than having to try and undo something which you have taught incorrectly.

The car.

It is at this stage of training, that you will probably be using the car to take the dog to a variety of different places to train on your own, or in the company of others. It is the time when, if you have not done it before, you should start gaining some control in terms of how and when a dog gets in and out of the car safely and on command.

When puppies are very small most have to be lifted into and out of the car, but once they have grown, and are able to jump in and out of a car on their own, then that is the time when they want to do just that – in or out when they decide to! Handlers should be aware of this stage which is usually when a puppy starts to realise that the outing is exciting and something they want to do.

Hopefully your puppy will have got used to travelling in the car and you will have ensured that he is always put into the boot area, preferably in a suitable dog cage. I do not believe in dogs travelling in the interior of the car at any time as I believe it is unsafe for the puppy, but probably more importantly, is unsafe for all other occupants of the car. Dog cages can be bought relatively cheaply and, from a safety point of view, are well worth the expenditure. I have also found that dogs seem much more contented and secure in a cage.

A cage too, allows the boot door to be opened without danger of a dog jumping out, but also allows on a hot day for example, the boot to be left open when the car is parked and therefore puts the dog at less risk from exposure to heat, which can result in death very quickly when a dog is left in the car without adequate ventilation.

Taking control of a puppy or older dog in matters associated with the car is no different from taking control in other circumstances, once you have taught the dog what he must do to obey your commands.

It is a simple task for a dog to obey a sit command wherever he is.

It appears that it is not such a simple task for a handler either to give a sit command to a dog when about to get into or out of a vehicle, or to ensure that this command is obeyed.

The life of the dog could be at stake when considering all the possible problems which could occur and the risks involved when a dog is near traffic or going to areas away from home when who knows what dangers may be lurking not only to the dog, but dangers to livestock and humans from your dog.

Car exit and entry training.

You and the dog need to be at the stage where you can put a lead on the dog without any struggling. This means that you are not having to grab the dog and wrestle to get the lead on. If this is not the case, then you should sort out this problem first.

The dog should have been taught, and has learnt, what the 'sit' command means and is beginning to understand that 'sit' means 'sit' no matter where he is, no matter what you are doing and no matter what may be happening around him. That is *sit no matter what....*'

I find the best way of beginning to take control of the dog concerning the travelling arrangements, is at the stage when the dog is already in the car. You begin, therefore, at the point of taking control of the dog getting *out* of the car.

When you first start this training you need to make sure you have plenty of time. The dog should not be allowed to get out of the car until and unless it is in a controlled manner, on command. You should therefore make this a training session in its own right, rather than try to rush it when time is limited. Some dogs grasp the training in minutes, but others, either those who have been allowed to leap out of the car the minute a door is opened, or those who have had to be physically restrained to prevent them leaping from the car, may take a lot longer to grasp the new rule.

As soon as you decide to start this training your dog should never again leap out of the car until he is allowed, on command, to do so; similarly he will never again be allowed to leap into the car until allowed, on command, to do so.

The following steps assume that the dog is in a cage which is in the boot area of the car:

- Open the boot door.
- Give your dog a 'sit' command followed by a 'good boy' when he obeys.
- Open cage door slightly, whilst reminding dog 'sit, good boy'.
- If the dog remains in a sit, the cage door can be opened fully, but you must keep the dog in a sit. Be ready to shut the cage door if the dog even looks as though he is going to get out.

Taking Control

- 🐾 Continue to remind the dog 'sit, good boy' and place the lead on the dog. The dog should remain in a sit and you should be ready to close the cage door, if there are any problems.
- 🐾 Once the lead is on the dog, step away from the car whilst the dog remains in the sit position.
- 🐾 Wait for several seconds whilst continuing to remind the dog 'sit, good boy' and, when you are ready, give the dog a command, of your choice, to get out.
- 🐾 Once the dog has got out of the car, on command, he should then be given a 'sit' command and should remain sitting whilst you close the cage door and close the boot door.
- 🐾 You can then give the dog a 'heel' command and walk away.

Once you decide to start this training, it is vital that you do not allow the dog to get out of the car until commanded to do so, and you need to take your time over it. If the dog, despite your best efforts, escapes or jumps out at any stage, the best way is simply to get hold of the dog and put him back in the car. You should not talk to the dog other than giving a growl, at the time he jumps out. Do not give any commands or say anything. Simply put the dog back into the car, calm down, take a few deep breaths, and start all over again.

What you should not do at this stage is say 'oh well, he's out now, we'll forget it this time and try again tomorrow'. Tomorrow will be worse than today, so if you have decided that 'today I am going to teach the dog that he can only get out of the car when I say so, on command', then that is what should happen, however long it takes!

So far, of course, you have only taught half of the procedure. Your next task will be to teach the dog that he is only allowed to get into the car when you say so, and on command. Having achieved the first part of this training you will find that this part is somewhat easier for most handlers, and with the majority of dogs. For a start the handler has actually got the dog on a lead, and a lead should always ensure that a handler has the last word on any subject concerning the control of the dog!

When you are ready therefore, proceed as follows:

- Approach the back of the car with the dog on a lead in the heel position.
- Command the dog to 'sit' and ensure the command is obeyed instantly by the dog, or by you positioning him. Praise the dog for obeying.
- Keeping the dog in the sit position, by constant reminders of 'sit, good boy', open the boot door and the cage door and be ready, should the dog move, to reinforce the sit either with reminders, or if necessary with a growl punishment for moving and another command to sit.
- The dog must not jump into the car. It is therefore necessary for you to be ready, to close the cage door or prevent the dog jumping up by restraining him on the lead.
- Take your time, and when the dog remains in a sit with the cage door open for a few seconds, then give him a command, of your choice, to jump into the cage.
- Once the dog is in the cage, you should give him another sit command, which he should obey.
- Once the dog is sitting in the cage, you should remove the lead and, whilst closing the cage door and making sure the dog cannot get out again, give the dog, the release command. (You need to release the dog because, although he is not free to go off on his own, because he is in the cage, he needs to be released from obeying your last command of sit. He can therefore choose for himself whether to sit, lie down or stand, within the cage.)

Having successfully achieved this, you should ensure that the same procedure is adopted for life. Each time you go out in the car with the dog, the process of controlled access and exit will be easier, and in a very short time, provided you are vigilant and consistent, you will find your dog will be sitting before getting into the car and before getting out, waiting for the permission to do each.

Most of the above, assumes that a dog *wants* to get into the car and wants to get *out* of a car too. I have come across several dogs recently which appear not to want to do either, in fact show a distinct reluctance to get into the car, and once in it, will show a reluctance to get out of it. All the problems I have seen, concerning getting into the car, have been totally created by the handler, mainly because the handlers have given the dog the choice.

If a handler gives the dog the equivalent of 'do you want to get into the car, or not?' question and the dog decides on the 'no I don't want to' option, handlers have then lifted the dog into the car, or in some cases allowed the dog to get onto some ones knee in the car, or into the main body of the car rather than in the boot.

I have no objection to lifting a dog into a car. I do it with puppies and I have done it with several elderly dogs, but it is my decision and not the decision of the dog in question.

Once you know a dog is physically, both strong and big enough to get into the car himself, and you decide 'today is the day I'm going to teach the puppy how to get into the car', then that is what should happen. I have never had to make one of my dogs do this, but have had to do it with a variety of pupils and the way to do it is that you must, on no account, give the dog a choice. This does not mean taking a punishment stance but it does mean that you will have to insist but usually you will only have to insist once or twice only.

With a reluctant dog, the exercise is best attempted from the opposite way, so begin with the dog out of the car, on a lead. Position the dog fairly close to the car and to begin it is preferable not to have the dog on a sit so do not give this command. Open the doors to the boot and cage. Standing close to the car yourself, give the dog your chosen command to get into the car once. Then by using the lead and, if necessary, putting your hand on the dog's lower rump, pull forward and upwards on the lead and simultaneously push upwards and forward on the rump. You must keep tight hold of the lead and ensure the dog does not get away.

When I have had to teach this to other people's dogs, all the dogs have already developed a phobia about getting into the car and immediately they sense some compulsion regarding getting in, they panic and try to escape. This is the point where you should ensure the dog gets into the car quickly and once in, you must give lots of praise. You should then try the reverse procedure of the exercise by closing the cage door, then opening it and putting the lead on the dog. Most dogs with this problem, I have found, do not want then, to get out of the car so there is no point in giving a sit command unless your dog only has a problem with getting in.

Once the lead is on the dog, give the dog your chosen command to get out. Give the command only once and then ensure the dog gets out, by pulling on the lead. Once the dog is out of the car, give him lots of praise, then give him a heel command and have a short walk round before going back to the car. You should then repeat the exercise as many times as it takes until your dog is, getting into and out of the car by himself, when you give him the command.

If you are determined, the dog will do it properly after a few attempts. It is important that you do not give up before the dog obeys. I have never had a dog which needed more than 6 attempts before he was leaping in unassisted and that was with a dog of 5 years of age. This dog was a very large Labrador retriever which had been lifted into the passenger well of the car all his life because 'he has always been frightened of the car'. The dog was not frightened at all. He had simply found a brilliant way of ensuring the whole family were inconvenienced by his behaviour and he got what he wanted, which was a cushion covered with some vet-bed, a pile of biscuits, and 'life was very comfortable, thank you'. The dog would have been an idiot to change his behaviour voluntarily!

He had never been taught to get into the car, had no way of knowing the rest of his pack wanted him to get into the car and his behaviour had become a ritual with the four members of the family, until he met me! The dog was not difficult or unresponsive. It took only 4 attempts to teach him and another 2 attempts with him doing it by himself perfectly. He then did it properly with the two adult members of the family and never again sat in the front. This improved the life of everyone. The dog was in a safer place and the mother and two teenage children could then have a seat each instead of all being crammed into the back seats because, 'Jason, sits in the front'!

Once a dog has been taught to get in and out of a car on command, he should, having been given the command, not be allowed to disobey it. Most dogs get the message very quickly, particularly with the association of training classes, or going somewhere exciting, and most dogs also get the message very quickly that, 'we are not going anywhere mate, until you behave yourself!'

Correct behaviour in relation to the car and travelling is more than another exercise in training, it is the safety drill, the emergency instructions and the life-saving procedure all rolled into one, and the dogs' life could depend on you getting this right. More importantly you could be putting other people and other animals at risk if you do not take control of this aspect. If you do not take control, you will not have control.

❀ (h) Taking control of exit from the car

(Left) Start with the dog in the car. Open the boot, give the dog a 'sit' command and then open the cage door.

(Right) The dog must remain in the sit position, inside the cage, with the door open.

(Left) The lead should be put onto the dog but the dog must remain sitting in the cage.

Taking Control

(i)

(Left) Give the dog a command to jump out and then give the dog a sit command.

**(Below) The dog should remain in a sit position whilst you close the doors of the cage and boot.
You should then give the dog a heel command and walk away a short distance before returning to the car to practice entry to the car.**

❀ (j) Taking control of entry into the car

(Left) Approach the car with the dog on a lead and give the dog a sit command.

(Right) The dog should remain in the sit position, on a loose lead, whilst you open the doors of the boot and cage.

(Left) Give the dog a command to get into the car, give the dog a 'sit' command and remove the lead. The dog should remain in the sit position with the cage door open.

(k)

(Right) The cage door should then be closed, the dog given the release command, and finally the door of the boot should be closed.

(Photographs: Mary Ward)

The demonstration photographs show a puppy of 8 months old.

☢ (l) Water experience with a puppy aged 9 weeks

Show the puppy the water and let her experience it.

Tasting it is part of the fun!

(m)

'Perhaps I'll get in it'

'Oh look, I found this'

(Photographs: Paul Lawrence)

Demonstration photographs are of a puppy aged 9 weeks.

CHAPTER SEVEN

Water experience

All dogs have the natural ability to swim and most of the Retriever breeds love swimming and anything which involves water. For the majority of gundog breeds, if they can get themselves wet or dirty – the muddier the better, it is fine as far as they are concerned. They even prefer drinking muddy water rather than clean water from a more hygienic dish!

Having the inbuilt ability to swim does not however, mean that all dogs will actually swim, on command, whenever you want them to do so and giving a dog water experience should be an essential part of everything else a young dog is learning in the early months. It is important to bear in mind that a handler at this stage is not aiming to teach a dog to swim on command, neither is it the purpose to try and get dogs to swim at all. This learning opportunity is to give the puppy experience of water and nothing else.

There are several ways to introduce a young dog to water; often people let pups play around water with other dogs or throw things into water so a puppy swims without realizing that they are so doing. I have tried all sorts of ways and all seemed to work until I had a puppy who would not swim. I realized then, that previous ones would probably have swum, whatever the method of introduction, but that reluctant ones may well be put off by these methods. This particular puppy used to stand and bark at other dogs swimming, telling them in no uncertain manner, to come out or they would drown! Since then I have always structured introduction to water, believing that it is better not to leave things to chance.

The first consideration needs to be the weather. If you are giving this experience at home with a suitable water container, choose a warm day. If you have to go outside the home to find a stretch of suitable water it is better to choose a day when the water temperature is reasonably warm. I don't think the time of year matters because the water on a wet, winter day is quite good. The second consideration should be the age of the dog. The younger the better! If you can give a puppy of around 12/13 weeks some water experience, they seem to take to swimming without any fears and accept it as just part of everything else they are seeing and doing for the first time. It has to be remembered that this is experience of water and not experience of swimming and it should be thought of as play, similar to the way young children experience playing with water with toys; getting their hands into it to feel texture and the properties of water where they need to get wet, feel it, taste it and experience all the wonders of it.

Ways of providing water for a young puppy could be a child's paddling pool with a few inches of water or even a large washing-up bowl, anything which a puppy can get into and explore. Plastic dog beds are good – the ones with an opening at the front will take 3 or 4 inches of water. **Don't let puppies be alone – you should always stay with them if they are with water.**

All you need to do is put a suitable receptacle outside. Let the puppy watch you doing it, put a few things into the water such as a floating plastic bottle, a dog toy, or anything which may attract the puppy to investigate, but which will not harm the puppy. If you start playing with the items, holding the water in your hands, splashing it around, most puppies will want to get involved. Your puppy may not get into the water but the aim will be to get him to relate to it in some way. Many young puppies, feel they should drink it. This is quite normal because this is all they have done with water up to this point.

Whatever the puppy does, take the water and toys away after a few minutes. This is a special thing that only happens for a short time, now and again. Repeat the experience a few days later and you will find that every puppy will do more the next time. You will find after a few sessions that the puppy will be trying to get into the water before you get the receptacle on the ground. This is an indication that things can be taken a little further.

You may find that if your puppy gets wet, even if he is only wet on his paws or other small areas, he will shake to get rid of the water. This is an ideal opportunity to start teaching the puppy a valuable command of 'shake'. At present, the puppy will not understand what the word means, but if you say the word 'shake' when he is in the process of shaking, you will eventually be able to say the word when the dog *is* wet, and he will shake *on command*. This may seem of little consequence at the moment, but is another valuable command which you will need later when your dog is retrieving from water.

Once a puppy has started to learn some heel work on a lead you can try and find some water, perhaps away from home, where a young puppy can play and run through shallow water and splash around. Streams and large puddles are ideal and I also find flood water in a field a good place to start. A pond or lake will also be suitable provided there is something like a beach area or shallow entry of some sort. Even bold puppies may frighten themselves if they suddenly plunge into deep water. Most dogs seem to know instinctively when water is deep, even older dogs experienced in swimming, are sometimes reluctant to swim in extremely deep water. Make sure, by walking in the water yourself, that it is only a few inches deep.

For the first session let the puppy play. You may need to be in the water yourself, holding it in your hands, splashing it around, but essentially you should let the puppy learn about it, in his own way being careful not to do anything other than make it fun and make sure your puppy is not frightened. You should avoid physically putting the puppy into the water and sometimes puppies will not go into strange water the first time. If this is the case, do not try and force the issue, simply go home and try again a few days later.

If your puppy is happy with going into water at home and then into water away from home, (you may need to return to the same place several times but just keep going every so often) you will find that the puppy, provided no pressure is put on him, will be more adventurous every time. After a few sessions you will find that the puppy enters water himself, many will be happy to run through shallow water and often they appear not to notice that they are in it. I never throw things in water at this stage but having a rubber toy or plastic bottle to float, is a good idea, then the puppy can play in water and get used to the feel of it splashing and get used to putting his mouth into the water for a toy.

You can get some very attractive rubber and plastic bath toys, designed for babies, which are ideal for puppies. They float, they are in bright colours and most are easily picked up by a small puppy, making them ideal for these first water experiences. Even at 12 weeks, some of the bolder puppies will swim if the water is a little deeper than paddling depth but this should not be forced. Make the first water sessions fun and your puppy should have no problems later, because they remember that it was good experience rather than a frightening one.

You should never throw a puppy, or older dog into water and I believe you should never even place a puppy into water. If you stay relaxed the puppy will work it out in his own time, at his own pace.

This is all that is necessary for water experience to begin. Once the puppy is confident you can try taking him to a larger pool but don't try and make him swim, just let him play in the same way as before. The confident ones may well swim and the less confident can play and remain happy with the experience.

I don't do any formal training with water after this, until I have some control. Wait until you get to the stage of the dog knowing 'hold', 'give' and doing a 'marked retrieve'. Then, introduce water, along with increasing the dog's experience of other types of terrain such as woodland, long grass, stubble and every other type of area which will increase the dog's experience and skills.

With older dogs, if they have had no water experience, it is useful to follow the same pattern as with a puppy and let them play and experience water. Older dogs who have had water experience and are swimming, often before they have learnt any commands and before their handler has *taken control*, frequently become 'water idiots' and like nothing better! These are the dogs which will probably cause you problems in gundog training so try and keep them away from water until you have control and they are at the stage of retrieving a 'marked dummy.' If a handler has no control over the dog on land, they stand no chance at all once the dog is in a lake!

Dogs whose idea of Heaven, is water, have the most stressed handlers! It is the most difficult place to maintain control of a dog so both of you need to get on with your other homework first!!

❧ (n) Exploring and having fun with water away from home.

(Photographs: Anthea Lawrence)
Puppies 4 months of age, exploring water on a water training course.

✦ (o) The 'leave it' command

(Left) This young Labrador retriever (14 weeks) has begun to learn what 'leave it' means: consequently she turns her head away from the dummies lying on the ground, to avoid temptation.

(Below) Puppies in class sitting whilst dummies are thrown. These puppies have leads on but the handlers have dropped the lead onto the ground

(Above) Golden puppies (20 wks.) Off the lead but leaving tennis balls placed in front of them.

Taking Control — 85 —

(p)
Puppies in class sitting quietly after dummies have been thrown, remaining in a sit whilst a handler goes to pick up a dummy.

The handler then returns to his dog, demonstrating the correct way to return, which is round to the right of the dog and back into the heel position.

CHAPTER EIGHT

The 'Leave it' command

Many people feel that a Retriever breed or other gundog breed, whose role includes retrieving, does just that – retrieves. Now whilst this may be true as a general statement the crucial part left out, by many, is that the retrieving should be *on command* and in fact most gundogs, whether it is their primary function or not, spend most of their time *not retrieving*.

Most gundogs from working stock have an instinct to retrieve, having been bred from generations of dogs selected for the purpose but the last thing most people want is for this instinct to be given free reign which when coupled with a natural chase instinct, would mean that a dog would retrieve for its own benefit only. These instincts were after all, for the sole benefit originally of all dog packs because without them, the pack would not eat.

A gundog handler needs a dog to retrieve for the handler, to bring back everything retrieved to the handler and to hand over the resulting mouthful willingly with no resentment and no indication that the dog would prefer to keep or eat or bury or destroy whatever he has retrieved.

Puppies when with their dam and litter siblings learn a great deal about taking possession of things and keeping them for themselves or relinquishing them to a more powerful associate as this is all part of gaining essential survival skills and finding their place in the hierarchy of a pack. Part of their socialisation should concern dealing with humans in these early weeks and humans, need to be in charge of all play items as well as in charge of all dishes and food. These are the building blocks upon which early, more formal training is based when a puppy joins a new family, a new pack.

All humans, even quite small children from 2 years of age, should be in a higher social position than a dog and as such, I believe a dog should never think he owns anything or can take possession of anything which he will not allow a human to take. That does not mean that I believe children or adults should continually take things from a dog but they should be able to do so, if necessary and part of that training also involves acting *before* a dog has taken possession or before a dog has decided to do something inappropriate.

The command 'Leave It' is the one I use to convey to the dog that it can't have whatever he is looking at, at the time. It also means to the dog that he cannot do whatever he is thinking of doing at the time. Other commands will be needed for when a dog actually has something or is in the process of doing something which you do not want him to have or continue doing.

The definition of 'Leave It' to the dog is:

Dismiss from your mind all thought of having or doing what you are *thinking* of taking possession of, or getting involved in.

Many people have difficulty in understanding this, particularly the *'thinking'* aspect and it therefore needs some explanation in case any one feels I am expecting you all to develop skills in crystal ball gazing so that you can see into the future and guess what a dog is going to do!

I believe that almost everyone from 10 years of age can anticipate what a young child may be going to do with very little experience or training. It is almost an instinctual, reflex action to put a hand out to save a child from falling or to act in an appropriate fashion when a child is about to do something dangerous or which the older human has possibly learnt may not be a good idea, for a variety of reasons. We can all see into the future and can all take action to try and prevent, our split-second guess as to 'what happens next', turn into reality.

We read the signs and without thinking further, we react. We are not always right and some may jump in when it was not necessary but, whenever we react in this way we have not made a 'let me sit down and think about this' type of decision. Actions taken as a result of careful consideration may also be concerning safety and prevention but they involve a plan, a 'how can I improve this, or how can I prevent that?'

Teaching a dog 'Leave it' involves the latter but its implementation looks like a reflex action. That is we carefully plan, but make it look in practice as though it is an immediate reaction to danger.

In the process of training a dog, there are many things which we have to teach which involve our language in terms of words but also hand signals and our body language. Dogs are learning it as a foreign language but they also have a language which we need to learn about as much as possible, and on occasions utilise to our advantage. I wrote earlier about using a growl sound to indicate disapproval to a dog – this is using their language.

The 'leave it' command is the only exception to my rule that *all commands should be spoken in a normal, pleasant voice* and it is an exception because it is a *de*mand as opposed to a *co*mmand and should therefore be spoken as though a child is just about to step of a cliff top with a 200 feet sheer drop in front of him. You would shout **'NO',** or something else, not because you have thought about it, but because it is that split second reaction to danger. The 'LEAVE IT' command should be said loudly and in a horrible voice as it is used as a punishment.

It is the opposite of most commands in that most commands learnt are 'you must *do* this when I say a particular word'. The 'Leave it' command is a 'you must *not do* what you are thinking about doing'. In this way it is also a punishment, but different from the general meaning of punishments in that it is not a punishment for *doing* or even *not doing* something but is a punishment for *'thinking of doing something'* and it has to be a punishment in order to prevent the doing. If we go back to thinking about a child on a cliff top, shouting may frighten them, but you want to stop the child taking the next step which would plunge them to their death.

It would be no good punishing after the event, as it would be too late; the inevitable will have happened!

Personal space.

The personal space of a human is about 2 feet. Humans start to feel their personal space is being invaded if another human comes closer than 2 feet away and, depending on the circumstances, may feel happy if the space is invaded due to a personal or intimate relationship or uncomfortable because the invasion may threaten them. Their reaction then is to back away and try to retain the 2 feet margin or go further and get away all together. The personal space of a dog is much larger than that of a human and is about 6 feet. Anything, any person, animal or object approaching the dog's personal space and the dog is weighing it up.

The dog has 2 choices: if the thing approaching appears greater in some way than his ability to deal with it he runs away and tries to maintain his personal space, or make it even larger; if he can cope in some way with the thing approaching he thinks something along the lines of 'one more step mate and you're in MY area and anything in my area is MINE'. There is not anything, necessarily which would indicate aggression in this thinking, but aggression is one of the options (fight or flight).

This thinking is legitimate on the part of the dog. It is one of the survival instincts necessary to protect the individual as well as ensuring the well being of the pack and its continuity. It is not however, an instinct which will be totally useful in the dog's life as part of a human pack and is certainly not useful to handlers who have to ensure that *they* control, under usual circumstances, what happens in the combined personal space of dog and handler when they are together.

With young puppies, according to their breeding, biddability and upbringing thus far, anything approaching their personal space will, usually, bring thoughts into the puppy's mind of playing with and investigating the invader. With older dogs however, and also with young dogs which have not had possession rules explained to them, there may be aggression thought about, if not actually acted upon. This is one reason why this particular aspect of training is useful early rather than late and is an extremely effective way of helping the puppy learn some important leadership issues, but perhaps of greater importance, it is to help new owners and handlers to understand that some issues should be dealt with before they become issues!

Training

I like to teach this command fairly early in a training programme once the dog has begun some heelwork and is beginning to make some progress on a sit as well as coping with turns in various directions with halts in the process of practicing heelwork on the lead. It is best started in a training group and the way I start to teach the command is with some handlers and dogs stationary and another handler and dog walking round weaving in and out of the others.

If the stationary dogs are observed in this situation, it will be noticed that most will not take a great deal of specific interest in the handler and dog walking round until they get roughly to within 8 feet of them. That is because the walking handler and dog is approaching the dog's personal space which is about 6 feet and one more step is going to take the approaching handler and dog into that personal space.

It is at this point (6-8 feet away) that a handler should say 'LEAVE IT" with the thought in mind of stopping whatever thoughts the puppy is thinking concerning his options.

Handlers need to remember that this 'leave it' is a punishment and it is a punishment for the dog even thinking that he has to deal, in some way, with the situation. If the 'leave it' is said in a loud voice it should startle the puppy and wipe out the thoughts of what he may have been considering. Most puppies will look up at their handler at this point, whereupon the handler should smile and say 'good boy'. Whilst this is all happening, the approaching handler and dog will have passed by.

Timing is the crucial aspect. With novice handlers the problem areas are:

- The 'leave it' is not said loud enough, or is said in a too pleasant 'please would you' type of voice.
- The handler waits until the approaching handler and dog are within the 6 feet area or have passed by. This usually results in the puppy jumping on the walking puppy and handler from the rear.

Neither of these is good practice. The 'leave it' should be shouted sufficiently to startle the puppy, in a voice which says 'I demand you do this' and it should be followed, immediately, with 'good boy' so that at the time the walking handler and dog are passing by, the handler is praising the dog and the dog is relaxing. If the handler waits until the walking handler and dog are already in the personal space area or have passed by, a puppy will usually jump on the other puppy when it is near, because he will be acting on his instincts to deal with the situation.

It should be remembered therefore that the command is used to wipe out the thoughts of the dog at that crucial 6 feet away point. Any later than this and the command is worthless because the puppy has already thought! Timing is crucial so that the 'leave it' is used at the correct moment, but also very importantly, that the 'good boy' is being used at the time the approaching handler and dog is actually passing by, so that your puppy is concentrating on you instead of working out how to deal with the intruder in their space!

If there are several people in the group, by the time that everyone has walked round individually, most handlers manage to get the timing right, and with young puppies, they get the message very quickly.

It is useful at this stage to reinforce this learning both for the handler and the dog, by going onto another exercise which involves the same command and therefore furthers the understanding of the use of the command.

The exercise I use is throwing dummies, tennis balls, toys, anything really which will probably interest the dogs and help them understand another concept in that if their handler has given them a command of 'sit' then a 'leave it' command that they have to obey both commands simultaneously. It is also part of the dog beginning to understand that 'sit' means sit no matter what……..!

The exercise is fairly easy to set up:

- Have all the handlers either standing in a circle or in a straight line with the dogs sitting at heel.
- The person throwing the items should shout 'mark', tap the item on their hand and then throw it onto the ground. At this point it is better to ensure the items do not fall closer than about 2 or 3 feet from the dogs.
- Handlers should be instructed that when they hear the 'mark' being shouted, then they should shout 'leave it' to the dog and immediately go into praise. This will mean that before the item has landed on the ground the dog will be being praised, will be looking at the handler and will not think of getting up in order to investigate, whatever has fallen on the ground.

Once the dog is beginning to understand this command, dummies, toys and tennis balls can be thrown much closer to the dog and even left on the ground immediately in front of the dog – but that is for later. For the first experience of the command the above two exercises should suffice.

Further developments can then be as follows:

- Meet and Greet. To develop the exercise of several handlers standing with their dogs at heel on a sit, and one handler walking round; the walking handler and dog can stop in front of the stationary dogs with the people having a short conversation and the dogs sitting close to each other, but not interacting in any way.
- The above exercise can be further developed by each handler stroking the 'visiting' dog provided the 'visitor' remains at heel on a sit. Any jumping up, or moving, should be corrected by the handler and then the exercise tried again. The visiting dog should not be stroked until, and unless, he sits still and behaves properly.
- This exercise can then include both handlers stepping forward at the same time and stroking the dogs. Both dogs should remain under the control of their respective handlers. As additional control, it is also advisable for the person who is about to stroke another dog, to give that dog a 'sit' command, before stroking, and a further 'sit' command when they finish.

By the time you have had several weeks of teaching a dog the 'heel' and 'sit' positions and have made sure the dog understands both commands in all circumstances and the dog has also started to know what 'leave it' means, it will be time to take things a little further.

I have mentioned previously that the 'heel' and 'sit' commands must also begin to mean to the dog that the commands apply no matter what is going on around them and no matter what other people are doing and no matter what the handler is doing. Some of this *no matter what* is beginning to be understood by the dog in working, hopefully, in different places and with other people and dogs working alongside as well beginning to understand the 'leave it' command in relation to things happening in which they can take no part.

All this experience has occurred whilst the dog has been in the heel position and the dog will have begun to feel secure alongside his handler. It is at this point however that we need to be able to show and start teaching the dog that commands apply too when the dog is not sitting next to his handler.

Before you start this next step it is important that you have actually taught, and the dog has learned what the two commands of 'heel' and 'sit' mean and that the dog is obeying each of these commands instantly, on one command only, come what may and no matter what else is going on around. If the dog is not doing this, wait a bit longer and allow your dog to gain some more experience. Monitor yourself, look at why your dog may not be learning and either change things if you feel you have not been teaching correctly or just continue teaching the dog with patience.

I cannot give you a time scale for this because it differs with each dog and handler. Just be patient, take your time, and do not get cross. Sometimes a dog can appear to be learning very little of what you are teaching and then suddenly, overnight, he appears to understand everything all at once. It is important not to change the way you are teaching, provided you feel you are doing everything correctly, be patient, and go on teaching the dog in the same way.

Your next step will be to test the understanding of your dog in terms of what you have taught thus far concerning the two commands of 'heel' and 'sit' and see if your dog has actually learnt what you believe you have taught him.

The next two chapters concerning steadiness and gunshot should be read prior to this step however, as they give further information concerning why both these commands, and obedience to them, are so crucial.

Both are very basic, but without them there can be no further success or progress.

CHAPTER NINE

Steadiness

Steadiness is a term used by gundog handlers to mean a variety of things. It is a generic term which encompasses all the following:

- When walking to heel off the lead, does the dog remain in the correct position regardless of anything else going on around? In practice this could mean if you are walking with your dog, in the heel position, off the lead and a rabbit suddenly appeared and ran down the track in front of you, would your dog remain in the heel position? A dog which remains at heel, ignoring the rabbit, would be termed steady. (It may be termed by some, as a 'miracle'!)
- If you are standing with your dog sitting, off lead, in the heel position, does the dog remain sitting no matter what else is happening around? In practice this could mean if you are standing at a drive at a shoot and a shot bird lands quite close to your dog, would your dog remain sitting? A dog remaining in the sit position would be termed steady.
- Steadiness means obedience in that if you have taught the dog to do, or not to do something, have taught him how he should obey certain commands, is the dog obedient to those commands? Does the dog carry out your commands in all circumstances, despite what he may prefer to do? If he does this, he is steady.
- Steadiness also means whether you have given the dog sufficient experience to obey your commands under as many different circumstances as possible so that the dog is beginning to control himself without you having to keep nagging him all the time? A dog which acts appropriately, and immediately, without a handler having to command him continually or remind him, or if the dog takes an appropriate decision when the unexpected happens, will be termed steady.

In reality, you cannot have one of the above without all of them.

Although one could refer to a dog 'being steady' if it is seen to do any one of these things, it is the package of all aspects which is important.

Two terms used in gundog circles which are associated with steadiness are:

- (a) 'Running-in'. This is a description of an unsteady dog which, instead of waiting patiently at heel whilst walking or whilst sitting, sees a bird shot and runs in to retrieve it. He is classed as unsteady because he has not obeyed the 'heel' or 'sit' command given prior to the bird being shot and is therefore disobedient.
- (b) 'On the whistle'. This means that a dog is obedient to whistle commands usually meaning the sit/stop whistle, but could also mean the recall whistle. A dog which is 'on the whistle' is a steady dog.

Steadiness is a combination of training, temperament and experience, but it is perhaps the first and last of these factors which need to be dealt with in greatest detail, whilst the middle facet should only govern how the training and experience may be given and the speed of the progress.

How able a handler and/or an instructor is, in assessing the type of dog with which they are dealing, and therefore temper the training to suit, will also have a large part to play.

Steadiness does not just happen, but is an ongoing theme of everything which we teach the dog from the start. We can do everything we can to ensure the dog becomes, is, and remains steady but it requires constant attention. Unsteadiness on the other hand can usually be achieved with little effort, very early on and can remain a factor for life.

Much of the training and experience given to gundogs in the past was based on a decision to create unsteadiness in the beginning. The view held then, and is still the view of some today, was the one of waking up, or switching on and encouraging the dog's natural chase instincts. Puppies were therefore encouraged, and taught, to run after balls and dummies and were given lots of 'retrieves' long before any of them were taught and learned how to walk to heel, or sit.

When this more formal training started the dog would then have to be retrained or 'broken' of the habits they had learned. Depending on the expertise of the trainer, the temperament of the dog, and the nature or degree of the delight the dog has found in working for his own benefit, the breaking could be a difficult process which could lead to harsh treatment for a very dominant or wilful dog. For many novice handlers who tried to emulate methods used by professional trainers, the process of dog breaking was impossible. This resulted in many dogs being unsteady for life, or it meant that many dogs who may have led a useful and productive life were not able to be given this opportunity.

Today's thinking concerning the rights of animals coupled with more humane methods of training being developed, has resulted in many different ideas and techniques for teaching dogs what they need to learn. Many methods have, in my opinion, gone too far away from original dog breaking techniques and although such methods cannot be said to be physically harsh many still have far to go in their development towards a desirable finished product.

I believe that the majority of dogs want to please their handlers, want to be taught what is required of them and that it is unjust to teach a dog to do something for which later on I will punish him. I also believe it is unfair for a dog to be taught a system or learn types of behaviour that either a handler will later discard or the dog will be expected to discard.

For many people there was a need to get away from dog breaking techniques but unfortunately, even though many are not actively encouraging dogs to develop habits which will later have to be broken, many people have not replaced this period with anything else. A large number of people continue to believe that formal training should not begin until a puppy is between 6 and 12 months old. I really do not know why!

What I do know however, is that these are the dogs which are frequently brought to classes as adolescent hooligans having absolutely no respect for anyone or anything. It is unfortunate, and very sad, because most would have been delightful dogs if only their handler had decided to give them a proper education from the start.

What started as a realistic and commendable action to stop dog breaking techniques, is of absolutely no benefit to either mankind or the dogs if the resulting dogs cannot be trained using the variety of techniques currently available at the age where dog breaking would have been used.

My personal answer to this is to start when the puppy is young and start the way you mean to go on.

I therefore take a 'middle road' view of training in that I do not believe in physical punishment as a means of initial teaching, I believe in reward based teaching but I also believe that the lessons I teach, are for life. The rewards I use when the puppy is 8 weeks old will be the same rewards he will get, for life, and the things I begin teaching him at 8 weeks coupled with all the subsequent things I teach him during our life time together will remain my requirements of him, for life.

I will not encourage a dog to do something and then punish him for it later, how unjust that is! Neither however, will I reward a dog in such a way, for example by titbits, in order for him to learn something and then say the equivalent of, 'oh, good, now you have learnt what I want, you're not going to get the titbit anymore', as that too is unjust in my view.

This may seem a long way away from the point of 'steadiness' training, but as I believe in teaching a dog exactly what I require right from the beginning, steadiness has to be the theme running through all the separate aspects of formal training, but it must also be the theme running through all aspects of a dog's life which could lead to inadvertent learning by the dog. By this I mean that you may teach a dog inadvertently, that you require some types of behaviour from him due either to you rewarding him in some way for doing something you will later require him *not* to do, or because you have provided an opportunity for him to learn something for himself, which is not on your list of 'desirable things I want my dog to do later'.

In the first of these categories this could simply be praising or rewarding the dog in some way, at a time when he was not doing what you want or at a time when he was doing something which you may not want him to do later. This often happens with young puppies that are very appealing and amusing. They have little endearing habits which may seem cute or funny and which you say 'ah, bless him, look what he's doing' or 'he's so funny, when he does that'. All of which give the impression to the puppy that you admire, and therefore want, the behaviour. Now whilst, whatever the behaviour is, may appear harmless and cute now, when the puppy is small and just an adorable bundle of fur, the same behaviour when he is a hulking great 4 stone animal in adolescence, may appear much less cute and adorable and in fact may be dangerous and certainly much less desirable.

In the second category, if you provide an environment whereby the puppy is learning for himself that there are all sorts of attractions in the big wide world, his portfolio will be being formed on the lines of, 'wow, now I've discovered about this for myself, I'm going to do it all the time, because I like it'. You can guarantee that the 'this' will be something you do not want him to do!

So, try and start as you mean to go on, and think carefully. If a puppy starts to do something you do not want him to do, stop him! This does not have to be harsh in any way as young puppies are usually easy to divert onto something interesting which is less undesirable from your view-point. So if he is about to do something for example, which you do not want him to do, say 'no', divert his attention, perhaps give him a toy, pick him up, move him away, but beware of getting into a chasing type situation with a puppy. If you cannot easily get to the puppy, or you are too late to divert his attention it is sometimes better to ignore the behaviour, but just be ready for it the next time so that it does not become a habit for him.

Environment is the key. Make sure that you provide an environment that is secure and safe but which also does not contain a mine-field of things or opportunities which will be in some way harmful either to the puppy, the environment he is in, or your future training and obedience requirements. This will mean the whole family attending to these matters and a puppy in the household is an ideal way to teach the whole family to be tidy and not leave precious, valuable or important items within reach of a puppy because I can guarantee that the puppy will find them!

Steadiness? Is all this to do with steadiness? Oh yes! Go back to the beginning of this section, if you still have doubts and then think very carefully. If you want to guarantee that your adult dog is *unsteady* then you should ignore all this. Instead you should throw balls for your puppy and let him run and fetch them; if he does something you don't want, praise him and give him a biscuit; if he runs away with your wallet and is chewing your credit cards run after him making a lot of noise. These three things alone will ensure he is *unsteady, disobedient, won't want to relate to people and will be difficult to train.*

The alternative is to guard your investment with care, treat your puppy like a vintage bottle of wine you have just bought! Nurture him and provide an environment which will enhance his chances of learning what is required of him, correctly, and your investment will mature and give a life-time of pleasurable experiences for you. It will also give your puppy a framework in which he too can lead a fulfilled life, safe and secure in the knowledge that if he obeys you, life will be wonderful and everything will be taken care of by his trusted leader.

CHAPTER TEN

Noise and Gun shot

Working dogs need to accept, eventually, the sound and scent of guns as part of their normal working day. Yes it will excite them and get them all 'fired up' ready for the action but it should not worry or frighten them or lead to any other behaviour which is beyond eager, anticipation and this anticipation should not, in turn, over-ride any other training and control. The sound of a gun shot should not trigger any noise from a dog that should simply acknowledge the sound but not begin to whine, bark or make any noise at all at any time during or after he has heard the shot/s.

Gun shyness or gun nervousness is a term used when a dog exhibits signs of fear of the sound of gun shot. There are degrees of fear however and some dogs show some signs of this on occasions with symptoms which may include shaking, panting, excess salivation, tail clamped between the legs, ears flattened back to the head and crouching body posture. Provided the dog shows no other signs of fear, and the dog is quite prepared to work, adhere to all his obedience training and in particular will go towards the sound of the gun shot and retrieve if necessary, then this would be classed as nervousness and usually this disappears in time. It is important that if a handler notices any of these symptoms that they ignore them and carry on as though it is a perfectly normal situation.

Any acknowledgement to the dog, particularly if a handler tries to reassure the dog by praising or stroking him at a time when he is anxious will reinforce the dog's view, that it is something to worry about and he is right to be frightened. Handlers should be very careful therefore not to reinforce inappropriate behaviour by the dog which would, in turn, create an even bigger problem.

This type of behaviour is not true gun shyness, which usually has more intense symptoms of fear, usually accompanied by an inability to go anywhere near the sound of the shot and most often, the dog will in fact run away and/or hide.

Most working bred dogs do not exhibit signs of gun shyness or gun nervousness but this is a facet of training which needs to be taught with care and introduced as with all other facets of training so that a dog learns to accept and therefore treat as normal, scent of shot and the sound of gun-fire. It should also be scent and sound which whilst being normal, also excites and is viewed as a prelude and accompaniment to the activity.

Nothing, which is part of a gundog's training, should be taken as an entirely separate entity but a link or step towards something else. Each step of training needs to be carefully choreographed to take account of age, maturity, skills and training to date. Each step carefully incorporated into a previous stage with no clearly defined mark or line, which distinguishes where one piece ends and another piece, begins. In this way, when the end product is viewed, there will not, or should not, be any gaps or even join marks!

Training, regarding loud or strange noises starts during a puppy's critical period of socialization, which is at about 3 weeks of age until they are 3 months old. It is during this period that pups are beginning to become aware of their environment outside their whelping box. It is crucial that puppies are given the opportunity to encounter as wide a range of people, noises and smells as possible, having regard to their age and safety and it is also important to make sure that the mother of the puppies is not a nervous type who could well pass on fear responses inappropriately to her offspring. Puppies which are well socialized in these early weeks by their dam together with appropriate attention from the breeder are then much less likely to have problems later in life. These early experiences are essential, an important responsibility for breeders and an important information factor which prospective owners should address when viewing puppies.

If a puppy leaves it's breeder home at 8 weeks having been accustomed to normal household sounds such as domestic machinery, people with different voices, things dropping onto floors, noise of metal food bowls, children shouting and playing, radios and all manner of every day domestic sounds they will have become accustomed to these. The puppy will have learnt that although a sound may be loud, frightening or strange at first, the sound itself did not bite him or swallow him up or physically harm him and therefore can be viewed with caution but need not be worried about unduly.

Prospective owners should be wary of buying a puppy if the mother or the puppies appear to be hiding when visitors arrive and are reluctant to socialize. Normal, healthy puppies at around 4-6 weeks and older should be eager and willing to see you and scrambling over each other to be first. The mother of the puppies should be equally friendly and show no resentment in you seeing the puppies or a reluctance to let you talk to and pet her.

New owners need to be aware of the factors required to further a puppy's socialization period and therefore continue a puppy's education in these matters by being aware of the puppy and its many needs but not changing normal family life or trying to shield the puppy from the sound of the washing machine, TV or any other noises which are normal in and around any household.

The critical period of sensitivity in a puppy occurs between 8 and 12 weeks, so any experience causing acute fear, being hurt or stressful isolation during this time, may make a puppy fearful of such situations for the rest of its life. A careful balance therefore needs to be achieved of introducing variation of experiences but not to create fear. The aim being to reach the stage at about 3 months of age, when a puppy will view a new sound or experience with some caution but with curiosity and a healthy wish to investigate or be interested.

This may, to some people, seem far from the subject of gunfire, but I will return to statements made concerning any and all problems in training, and that is *'the solution to any problem, never lies at the point where the problem is seen or encountered'*.

Care in choosing a puppy from the type of breeder home where the *total* needs of a puppy are recognized and provided for, is crucial in prevention of gun problems, as too are factors such as choosing parents of a puppy which are well adjusted in all areas and making sure that the first few weeks and months of a puppy's life provide him with all the necessary experiences which are crucial to that period of his life.

Even when all the above factors have been addressed with care it will still be essential to consider how and when a gun type noise should be introduced into a training programme. I suppose one gets a feel for when this needs to be done and it is not always an easy thing to explain to others and my view is always leave it later, rather than introduce it too soon. I like to begin basic training and get to a stage where a puppy is enjoying the experience of working on simple basic exercises and enjoys and wants to be with and near me.

People can create a fear in a puppy simply by their attitude to something. A puppy picks up anxiety from our body language and because things seem different. If handlers view a shot as something about which they are worried, then they will appear tense, may grip the lead tightly or display inappropriate body language, all of which will transfer to the puppy whose senses will be 'on alert' and he will be in fight or flight mode and will just know that 'summat's up' and therefore something is going to happen which the puppy should be wary of too.

Training should have reached the stage where a puppy trusts his handler, knows the rules so far and is skilled in certain basic areas. The puppy will probably be at the stage where he is learning that 'sit' means sit, no matter what. The 'no matter what' will, to date, have included: a 'sit' whilst other dogs/handler move close to and past them; a 'sit' whilst a dummy is thrown or placed near them; and a 'sit' whilst another dog works. Heelwork should be being conducted in a variety of places and on a variety of suitable terrain, with none or few problems. If none, or not all, of this is true it is better to continue work on these matters before continuing further.

A shot noise can be introduced as a similar 'no matter what', and if handlers view it in this fashion, then the dog too will see this as another small bit of experience which is not going to harm him. It is important for handlers to view this stage as only part of the ongoing training situation, and not as a BIG event, whilst at the same time, taking care not to create problems. Many handlers are worried about gunshot and for novice handlers it is important to talk through how they should behave, which is to be relaxed and matter-of-fact about the situation. This is no different from any other training. For handlers who tend to be of a nervous disposition anyway, it is perhaps best to wait until their dog is at the stage of being steady off the lead at heel and will sit at heel off the lead whilst other things are going on and without showing any signs of running-in. In this way, the first gun shot experience can in fact be off the lead and there will therefore be no chance of a handler transferring any anxiety down the lead.

It is also important to talk through how a handler should react and how they should deal with any reaction in the dog. It is crucial that a handler does not inadvertently reward any fear response from the dog but should give verbal reward for an appropriate response by the dog.

Training

I always use a Starter Pistol for the first experience of a shot, for dogs of any age. Other choices would be a dummy launcher, without a dummy attached, or a shotgun, using blanks. Whatever the choice made, it is important that handlers never fire a shot themselves. If you are training your dog on your own, rather than in a group, you must make sure you take someone with you as well as teaching the other person what you require. I have known some previously well-adjusted puppies, which have been absolutely terrified by people taking them out and firing a shot close to their head or near them when the puppy was unaware that it would happen.

Many puppies never get over this fear inflicted on them by the person they respected the most at that time – their owner, their handler, their leader.

Many years ago, someone fired a dummy launcher about 2 ft. above the head of one of my puppies. I knew no better at the time, otherwise I would never have allowed it but, being a raw beginner myself, I trusted the instructor involved. This dog never ever recovered from this fright inflicted on her when she was approximately 5 months old. Possibly this was because I did not have the skills to deal with the problem then, but she was deeply suspicious of every thing and every situation regarding anything which could make a similar noise and she panicked regularly for the rest of her life.

There are puppies, of course, which will show no signs of worry no matter how or where they hear a shot and no matter how close, or how loud. As none of us knows however, whether we have a puppy who will have an adverse reaction or not, it is safer to err on the side of caution. Never put a puppy, or older dog, at risk by either firing a shot yourself, or allowing anyone else to fire a shot close to your dog. Care needs to be taken.

Having done some basic exercises, dogs should sit at heel on a loose lead or if they are already steady and/or the handler is not certain they will not jump or get nervous when the shot is fired, have the puppy off the lead in the heel position. At this stage of training most dogs will be used to seeing other people with dummy bags, used to seeing dummies being thrown and frequently they are all eyes and ears in anticipation of what is going to happen – 'they are up for it'!

There should not be anything secret about firing a pistol and the person who will be firing the pistol should stand near the dog/s to begin. If the person stands near by and spends time loading the blanks into the pistol the puppies will be watching, they will be gaining information from the sounds and the scents emanating from it. You can even let each puppy in turn sniff the loaded pistol. Once ready, the pistol firer should then walk away from the puppies and go as far away as possible to a distance which is still in sight and whereby the sound can still be heard. If possible, make sure the wind is coming towards the puppies from the pistol firer.

The pistol should then be fired once.

The ideal response is that dogs should turn to look where the sound is coming from and provided they remain sitting, the handler should give verbal praise of 'good boy'. (Praising for remaining in a 'sit', no matter what is going on around.)

The majority of puppies will act as above, look interested, sniff the air and relax with the verbal praise. If this is the case, then the pistol firer can be asked to move forward towards the puppies and fire another shot. For this first experience 5 or 6 shots may be fired with each shot slightly closer to the puppies but with the last shot at least 10 paces away from them. For the last 2 or 3 shots, throw a dummy after the shot with a handler leaving their dog in a sit whilst the handler goes to pick up the dummy. This will then be a known situation for the dog, combined with one new facet – the noise of the shot.

No further work needs be done with shot on that session but the training continue with other exercises. At subsequent sessions, shots can be fired a little closer or later on in the training programme, combined with a 'marked' or 'blind' retrieve. There is no need to use shot noises at every training session and no need to accompany every retrieve with a shot.

With young dogs they need to continue their basic training on all aspects, some of which later, on occasions, may have a shot.

If, despite very careful preparation and gradual build up as above, there is a problem with a puppy, or an older dog being introduced to shot, you will not be able to progress in the same way. It is difficult to say precisely what these problems may be and there would possibly be a different solution for each problem and each individual dog. I believe if there is an adverse reaction of any kind, with any dog, after one shot at a distance, or with shots a little closer, then no more shots should be fired after the point at which there was a perceived adverse reaction.

Monitor the dog carefully and try to understand what the dog is saying but be careful not to reward the dog or to punish either. To carry on with firing shots is a form of punishment if the dog is anything other than interested, but it is a form of punishment that will never lead to a correct behaviour from the dog and will in fact create a bigger, possibly incurable, problem. It is much better to continue with all other training and occasionally, get someone to fire a shot at a distance, in the same way as above. I have found it also useful with some dogs, to let them examine the pistol at close quarters. Put it on the ground near the dog after it has been fired and let the dog smell and explore it. Let the dog hold the pistol if he wants to, anything really which will make the dog more comfortable in dealing with it. Many dogs accept the sound much better after this, but it is always best to proceed with caution.

Once a puppy has no further reactions to one shot being fired at a distance, even if this takes many weeks or months, then you can start firing one shot, each time, a little closer.

Proceed with care and slowly, not moving on until the puppy accepts the noise and is unconcerned. A handler needs to be carefully monitored too just in case fear responses in the dog are being encouraged or triggered by a handler. If this is suspected, it is sometimes useful for someone else to hold the lead and let the puppy sit with another handler, or instructor, instead of his own handler and monitor whether the dog appears less worried. It may also be useful for the dog and handler to be engaged in an exercise which is known and liked by the dog, and arrange for one shot to be fired well away and out of sight, to see if it makes any difference. Most dogs are better if they can see what is making the noise, but others are better if they cannot see the source of the noise and therefore get acclimatised to it more easily.

Flow chart (2) - for the middle stages of training.

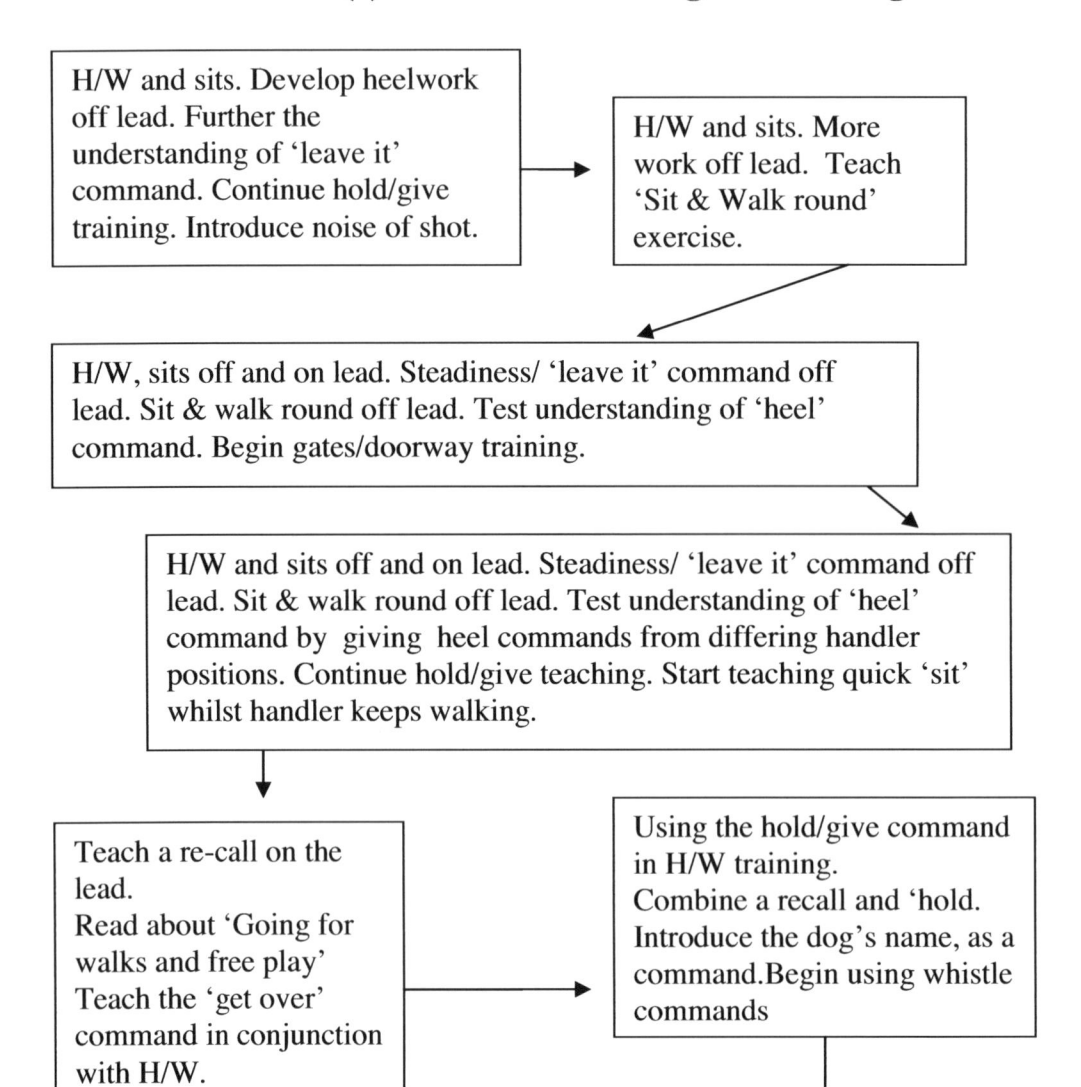

H/W and sits. Develop heelwork off lead. Further the understanding of 'leave it' command. Continue hold/give training. Introduce noise of shot.

→ H/W and sits. More work off lead. Teach 'Sit & Walk round' exercise.

H/W, sits off and on lead. Steadiness/ 'leave it' command off lead. Sit & walk round off lead. Test understanding of 'heel' command. Begin gates/doorway training.

H/W and sits off and on lead. Steadiness/ 'leave it' command off lead. Sit & walk round off lead. Test understanding of 'heel' command by giving heel commands from differing handler positions. Continue hold/give teaching. Start teaching quick 'sit' whilst handler keeps walking.

Teach a re-call on the lead.
Read about 'Going for walks and free play'
Teach the 'get over' command in conjunction with H/W.

Using the hold/give command in H/W training.
Combine a recall and 'hold. Introduce the dog's name, as a command. Begin using whistle commands

Check list:
1. Steadiness: Dog working off lead in H/W exercises amongst others and is steady to thrown dummies and other dogs working.
2. Dog has total understanding of the 'sit', 'heel' and 'leave it' commands.
3. Dog understands, and obeys, controlled entry and exit regarding the car and gates/doorways.
4. Dog understands a recall command.
5. The dog has achieved a 'hold' from the heel position and with a recall.

❦ (q) Gates and Doorways
Taking control at gates and doorways is an important part in determining the leadership role.

(Photographs: Mary Ward)

CHAPTER ELEVEN

Testing the understanding of heel and sit commands.

Once you get to the stage whereby your dog is walking to heel on a loose lead, will sit immediately you give the command and is beginning to understand the 'leave it' command, in that he continues to sit whilst another dog walks past or a dummy or tennis ball is thrown or left close by him, it is time to test whether the dog actually understands the commands you have been teaching him, as well as move his education on slightly.

You may be thinking that your dog obviously has learnt the commands because he is doing everything. Dogs sometimes learn more from situations in terms of our habits, what happens when we go to certain places, what happens when an instructor is present; than they learn about the one thing that we perhaps think we are teaching them. We need to test this and make sure, before moving on a few steps, that the dog has learnt and has an understanding in keeping with our own understanding of what we believe we have taught.

The sit & walk round exercise.

To begin teaching this new exercise it is best to do some heelwork and sit exercises first and make sure you have control and your dog is responding to your commands instantly.

For this exercise your dog needs to be sitting in the heel position on the lead. Up to this point in training, whenever you have stopped and given a 'sit' command, your dog has obeyed, you have praised him and the next command has been 'heel' and you have both set off walking again.

This is going to be something new and an opportunity for you to begin teaching the dog that he must not anticipate a command but must continue obeying one command until you give him another command. Handlers should have learnt their part in this all ready in that so far, whenever a halt has been made and a sit command has been given, the handler has always said 'heel' again before walking and expecting the dog to walk too! I said previously that this 'heel' command when setting off again after a halt was very important because later you would be walking and expecting your dog to remain in a sit position. Those handlers who have not been consistent with this are about to become unstuck! The 'later', has arrived!

Training.

When your dog is sitting in the correct heel position transfer the lead from your right hand to your left and put the surplus lead behind the dog, keeping your left hand near the withers (shoulder) behind the dog's head. Then say 'sit, good boy' to the dog and at the same time hold up your right hand in front of the dog and then withdraw it. This should get the attention of the dog on you and at that point you should take a step out to the right, remain there for a second, repeat the 'sit, good boy' command with hand signal and then step back into the heel position. Hopefully the dog will remain in position. If not, growl at him and just put him back where he was, take a deep breath and start again.

There is no point in getting cross, remember you are teaching the dog what you want him to do and you can only show him what to do by putting him back exactly where he was and following the same routine to the letter. Most dogs will remain where they are, some get up but most take no more than 5 or 6 times of getting up and being put back, before they know what to do.

When you can move one step away and your dog remains in position, then you can take it further: set up the exercise in exactly the same way but this time once you have taken a step to the side, then take a step out to the front as well before moving back to the heel position. If your dog moves, put him back and start again.

The aim is for the handler to be able to walk all the way round the dog from the heel position and back into the heel position without the dog moving. If you are patient, and help the dog by praising when he is correct, growling when he is wrong, putting him back and starting again, you could complete this exercise in less than 5 minutes.

Once you can take the steps to the side, then to the front, try again and simply walk all the way round but be ready to stop, growl, put the dog back into position and then try again. Once you have gone all the way round successfully, do not try the exercise again until your next training session. Let the dog think about it and you will find that next time you will be able to do the exercise from start to finish in a few seconds.

If you are working on your own and things go wrong there are several areas to consider as to likely cause:

- Have you been inconsistent in the past in terms of not always giving a 'heel' command after a halt with a 'sit'? If you have already taught the dog inadvertently that sometimes he has to go with you when you give him a 'heel' command and sometimes he has to go with you when you don't give a 'heel' command, you will need to spend a few more sessions on heelwork making sure you are totally consistent before trying the sit & walk round exercise again.
- Are you making sure you have the lead behind the dog's head and not pulling on it? Keep the lead behind the dog but also keep your left hand there too. The easiest way to do this is to pretend you are holding onto a post and then you walk round the post.
- Are you walking normally? It is surprising how many people walk in a strange way when starting this exercise. If you are walking as though you're trying to avoid stepping on eggs and breaking them, stop. Dogs sense something is wrong and therefore want to close ranks with you. Walk normally, walk

confidently, walk tall, expecting the dog to remain exactly where he is, because that is what you have told him to do.

- 🐾 Don't use any word but 'sit' together with praise words. It is surprising how many words people start saying when things go wrong and surprising how many words some people use which can make things go wrong. If the dog hears anything other than the command he knows with appropriate praise, he may get confused, think he has to do something in response to the words you are saying. This 'doing something' will probably mean the dog gets up.
- 🐾 Are you doing the exercise in exactly the same way every time you try to teach the dog? If you do anything different with some dogs they get confused so monitor yourself closely and don't assume you have a stupid dog but ask yourself, 'what am I doing wrong which is preventing my dog learning what I am trying to teach him?'

On this exercise you have begun to further your dog's understanding of listening for your commands and also to watch you at a distance. It is not a long distance at present but remember you are building foundations. You have also begun hand signals which, although the dog will not understand this immediately, your hand will become important for guidance.

In the same way as command words need to be used sparingly but consistently so that they have some impact, hand signals too should have some impact and it is at this stage that the dog begins to learn this. The hand signal should be used and the hand should then be put down, put away until the next time you need it. If you walk all the way round your dog with your hand remaining up, the dog will cease to pay attention to it, so do not be tempted to do this but use it sparingly and only in conjunction with your verbal 'sit' command.

You now have another exercise to combine with your short sessions of heelwork and sits and this exercise can now be used once or twice in each training session.

You should continue furthering the experience for your dog by doing training on the same things, but using as many different places to do them in as you can find and it is at this stage when it is useful to begin a small bit of heelwork with the dog off the lead. You need to do this gradually however and before starting make sure that your dog is already walking on a loose lead and that he is responding to a halt and 'sit' command instantly without you having to position him.

Start with some exercises as usual on the lead and then, after a halt and 'sit' simply wind the lead round the dog's neck and tuck the loose end in. In this way the dog is on the lead, but the handler is not! Then simply walk as usual giving a 'heel' command as you step out. Do not change anything else in terms of how you walk or what you do but remember to praise the dog continually, when he is in the correct position. Most people find that the dog simply does what he has been taught and the fact that he is no longer attached to the handler by the lead makes no difference.

It is important not to do too much, so if you can walk a few paces, do an about turn and two or three halts with sits, then that should be sufficient for the first time. Build up gradually on subsequent training sessions and eventually, if all is well, simply remove the lead all together, but remember to keep control by putting the dog on a sit first. All training sessions can then incorporate some work off lead and heelwork with different turns and halts as well as a few sit & walk round exercises.

You should continue to do as much on the lead as you do off the lead however at this stage and make sure you do not incorporate too many distractions which may tempt the dog to disobey you. Make an environment which encourages the dog to learn by ensuring as far as possible that the dog cannot go wrong.

Once you and the dog have a firm understanding of the sit & walk round and the dog is remaining steady off lead in all he has been taught, you can begin making a much larger circle round your dog when doing the sit & walk round exercise off the lead. Once this is achieved it can all be used as the start of numerous other exercises.

The first of these is used partly to test whether your dog fully understands what 'heel' means but is also a means of putting more distance between handler and dog and for the dog to begin to understand that the handler still controls everything even when not close to the dog.

Testing the understanding of the 'heel' command.

The heel command means 'be on my left hand side, 6 inches away, with your right shoulder parallel with my left leg' but it also means 'face in the same direction as me'. The recall command 'come' means return to me or come towards me but it also means 'face me' and it is an entirely different position for the dog to understand.

This may seem fairly obvious but it is surprising how many handlers do not understand the concept and unless a handler understands it, the dog will not be able to understand, mainly because a handler will often think the two words 'heel' and 'come' are interchangeable, which they are not!

The understanding and knowledge of the exact meaning of the two commands is crucial when a re-call is taught because the 'come' or other recall word used, will not only mean 'come to me' or 'come towards me' but will also mean 'face me' and this is totally different from 'heel' which also means 'face in the same direction as me'.

This exercise is simply an add on extra to the basic sit & walk round exercise already taught but takes it a little further and adds a different concept.

Training.

Start by doing a sit & walk round with the dog off the lead. Then repeat the exercise, but this time instead of going back into the heel position after you have walked round the dog, continue walking through the heel position until you are 4 or 5 paces out in front of the dog. You will need to remind the dog with a hand signal and a 'sit, good boy' when you pass through the heel position. It is important that you keep your back to the dog, so you will have to turn your body from the waist; to the left so that you can see the dog and the dog can see your face and your hand signal.

Wait a few seconds in that position but give one or two reminders of 'sit, good boy' with a hand signal and then, if your dog remains in position, simply look down at your left ankle and say one word 'heel'. Hopefully your dog will get up and start to move towards you. When the dog shows the first sign of getting up, say 'good boy' this is used as a 'yes, you are doing the right thing' encouraging praise. Do not look directly at the dog but continue looking at your left ankle and when the dog comes into your line of vision, say 'sit' with a 'good boy' when the dog obeys.

If anything goes wrong on this exercise, the best thing to do is stop. It should be immediately obvious where you need to do some more work and there is no point in trying to correct any area whilst in the process of this exercise. You will therefore need to continue for a bit longer on any area which appears to need some further training and this will be either some more heelwork on and off lead, more sit and steadiness exercises or attention to yourself concerning your consistency on commands, teaching and appropriate praise for when the dog is correct. Leave this exercise until you have put right any area where there was a perceived problem.

If everything went well you can be very, very pleased with yourself at this stage, as this will show you that you have been a good teacher and have successfully taught the dog several things:

- To remain steady and obey you at a distance, no matter what you are doing.
- He understands that 'sit' means *sit no matter what is happening around him.*
- He understands that he must continue obeying one command until you give him another command, and then he must obey the subsequent command.
- He understands where the 'heel' position is.

Well done both of you. Praise the dog; slip the lead on him and then you can give him a cuddle! Do not do anything else that session.

These concepts can be developed in subsequent training sessions to further the dog's understanding and experience.

To test the sit command later, you can start to give a 'sit' command when in the process of developing heelwork off the lead. This exercise is useful in giving you information about whether the dog is listening to you, has understood the command and is obedient. It is also part of teaching the dog a further development of obeying you *no matter what* you may be doing.

Do some heelwork off the lead, and provided all is well, give a sit command to the dog and you keep walking. You need to plan this and when about to give the command, discipline yourself not to falter in your step at all. Simply give the verbal 'sit' command, with a hand signal and *keep walking.* Ideally, your dog will sit instantly, in which case, praise the dog but keep walking for another few paces and then turn and go back to the dog, into the heel position and praise again.

If your dog does not sit instantly and carries on walking, you should growl and put the dog back in the spot where you gave the command initially, then repeat the 'sit' command and walk away. Try the exercise 2 or 3 times and if it still is not working properly, do no more that session. Let the dog think about it and try again a few days later. During this time, it is important for you to think why the dog is not responding to your command.

- 🐾 Is the dog sitting instantly during normal heelwork sessions? If not, go back to positioning and continue heel work exercises until the dog sits instantly, on the first command. Then try the exercise again.
- 🐾 Are you stopping, or hesitating when you try the exercise? If so, go out and practice without the dog, until you can discipline yourself to give the command and not stop or falter.
- 🐾 Are you saying the 'sit' command differently or in a harsh voice? If so, remember it is simply a 'sit' command and nothing should change in terms of your voice or your body posture which could indicate to the dog, 'this is something strange, frightening or difficult'.

Be determined that it will work, and it probably will.

Set off thinking the dog will not obey, and he will probably oblige you!

Once the dog sits instantly and you carry on walking, variations can be made after the 'sit' command:

- 🐾 Keep walking and then without stopping, give the dog a 'heel' command when at a distance. Keep walking. The dog should put himself in the correct position in relation to you and walk beside you.
- 🐾 Keep walking but make a variety of turns whilst the dog continues to sit. Keep reminding the dog 'sit, good boy' and then either return to the dog and praise, or give a 'heel' command when you are turned sideways to him rather than with your back to him. The dog should position himself correctly in relation to you and face in the same direction as you.

Success on all these exercises will give you a lot of information about your dog's understanding and whether you have taught him correctly.

Using the control aspects of the 'sit' and 'heel' commands.

Once you have taught your dog the important aspects concerning the heel and sit positions, the dog is beginning to understand several things about each command:

- What he has to do when he hears the command, which is to adopt the position he has been taught.
- When he has to obey the command, which is now, the instant he hears the command.
- The duration of the command, which is he must continue to obey the last command given, no matter what else may be happening around him, no matter what other dogs and/or people may be doing and no matter what his handler may be doing. Part of this learning too, is that he has learnt, 'OK off you go' or whatever your release command is, which has released him from obeying the last command given and he is therefore free to stop obeying that command.
- Who he has to obey. Working amongst other dogs and handlers will have helped your dog listen to you, locate your voice from amongst other sounds and start to understand that if you have said 'sit' and another handler says 'heel' that he remains sitting until you give him another command.

Gates and doorways.

One important issue regarding leadership is that higher ranking humans and animals in the pack should always go first! Many dogs like pushing their way to the front and just have to be first through doors and gates or down stairs and steps. Now is the time they should be taught that they cannot do this!

Once you have taken control, concerning obedience to some basic commands, it is time to reinforce your leadership position in that, if approaching some area such as a gateway or door which you and the dog are to pass through, then *you* need to go through this before your dog.

There is no point in trying this exercise before your dog understands that he must sit when you have commanded him so to do, and you are able to take a step or more away from the dog whilst he continues to obey the 'sit' command. Once this is achieved you can begin teaching this exercise, and once taught the rule should be applied for ever more.

Training.

- Find a suitable gate which can be opened and closed, and with space each side, for you and the dog to walk through and back again.
- Approach the gate with the dog on the lead and when approximately a yard away from the gate, give your dog a 'sit' command.
- You should then step forward and open the gate whilst the dog remains in the sit position.
- Remind the dog 'sit, good boy' and then step through the gateway and keep your back to the dog. Give 2 or 3 reminder 'sit, good boy' commands and then give your dog a 'heel' command.
- The dog should immediately obey the command, at which point you should praise (for starting to obey the command). Once the dog has arrived in the correct heel position, give him a 'sit' command.
- Your dog should continue to obey the sit command whilst you then move to close the gate. Return to the heel position, praise

the dog and then give a heel command and walk away with the dog, for a few paces.
- ☻ You should then do an about turn, and repeat the exercise going in the opposite direction.

This procedure should then be adopted for life and can be practiced on a variety of similar gates and doorways. When using different places for your training, numerous other situations may be incorporated into your routine. Later you may have to negotiate styles, fences and other obstacles and then, either the above method can be used or, in some cases you may have to leave the dog in a sit, off lead, for a longer time whilst you climb a style or get over a wall or fence. Provided you go first, the method of getting the dog over or through the obstacle to join you may differ. You may use a 'heel' command and keep your back to the dog, or may use a recall command and stand facing the dog.

Having taught the principle of 'The leader, goes first' you should not allow the dog to believe he is the leader and let him go first, other than in certain circumstances. These circumstances may occur later in training, when you may need the dog to negotiate some obstacle first – perhaps due to safety issues.

In these circumstances you may well give the dog a 'get over' command, put the dog on a sit, and then negotiate the obstacle yourself, but that is for much later.

At present the rule should be applied rigidly whenever you and the dog are to pass through a similar opening or obstacle including doors at home but it should also be remembered that this is for when you and the dog are both involved. Other situations, for example, letting the dog out into the garden from the house are a little different. If you are not going out too, the easiest solution is to give the release command when the dog goes out.

Depending on the temperament of the dog, this is usually sufficient.

With some dogs however, it may be necessary to build some control into this and building some control into the situation is quite a good idea for all dogs.

The way to do this is to give the dog a 'sit' command, and ensure that you are able to open the door, with your dog continuing to obey the 'sit' command. When the dog is sitting patiently, with you continuing to praise him, and with the door fully open, then simply give him the release command. If your dog disobeys the sit command, you should close the door, not let the dog go through, and simply repeat the exercise until the dog understands he will not go out until he obeys you.

It is useful to teach the dog this exercise and although it may not be possible for the procedure to continue all the time, due to being busy, others in the household not sticking to the routine and all sorts of reasons whereby it simply just doesn't happen, it is helpful if, now and again, you enforce the rule. It is also a convenient way to prevent any one entering the house, being leapt upon by the dog.

Taking control of a dog when people come to the house should, or could, become a habit for all the family and eventually you will find that the dog starts to control himself in these circumstances. When you have a puppy and are beginning some exercises amongst others, part of the training should include your dog learning that he should not leap up at other people. At home when someone calls at the house you can continue this training by giving your dog a 'sit' command and then, perhaps getting a visitor to say 'hello' to the puppy and scratch him on the chest, whilst the puppy continues to obey you and continue sitting. Keep a lead handy by the door, and you can then slip this onto the puppy, when necessary.

(r) Concentration – common faults.

(Left) The handler here is allowing the dog to pull; the handler is keeping a tight lead, instead of a loose lead, and he continues walking but with the dog deciding the pace. The handler is doing nothing to help the dog learn where the heel position is and is in fact teaching the dog that he may please himself entirely. None of this is desirable!

(Right) The handler has 'switched off' and is unaware his dog is facing the wrong way!

(Left) This handler has given the commands 'heel' and 'sit' but does not make sure the dog obeys, she is involved in watching someone else and 'forgets' her dog.

(s)

(Right) The handler has come to a halt, given his dog a 'sit' command but does not insist that the dog sits in the correct heel position. This is so unfair on the dog and the handler is wasting a valuable opportunity to teach his dog exactly what
is required.

(Left) A handler who is concentrating; making sure her dog obeys her, no matter what else is going on around; and a dog which is learning correctly what she is supposed to do.

(Photographs: Mary Ward)

CHAPTER TWELVE

The Recall

To begin teaching a recall a dog needs to have made some progress on learning a 'sit' command and will have learnt to sit whilst on the lead and off the lead whilst you walk round him and return to the heel position and will have learnt to sit off the lead whilst you walk in front of him and then give him a heel command. Your dog should now be obeying the commands taught so far, speedily and on the first command given and you should not now be needing to position the dog other than when necessary, occasionally. If any of the above is not true, then you should spend a little longer on these aspects first.

I use the word 'come' as the command word for the re-call but you must choose your own word for the command and then use it consistently. Some people use the words 'front' or 'here' (the latter is difficult because it sounds like 'heel' and should only be used if another word instead of 'heel' is used for the heel position.)

I shall use the word 'come' throughout.

The definition of the recall command to the dog is: return to me as quickly as you can.
Command word – Come.

Training.

To teach a recall you need your dog on a lead. This exercise begins in the same way as the sit & walk round.

To teach the recall, do a sit & walk round once, in the usual way. Then, repeat the exercise but instead of stopping when you return to the heel position, walk through the heel position and walk a pace in front of your dog. Turn round to face the dog and remind the dog with a verbal 'sit, good boy' and with a hand signal. Wait for a few seconds whilst repeating the 'sit' command, with praise, to remind your dog to continue doing what he has been told to do. This should happen 2 or 3 times whilst you are waiting. If your dog remains sitting, remind your dog once more and then return to your dog by going to the right hand side of the dog, walk round the back of the dog and then back into the heel position and praise him.

Repeat the whole exercise and this time, when you are standing in front of the dog, remind him of the 'sit' 2 or 3 times as before, with praise, then say one word 'come'. Your dog should come immediately. If he does not come immediately you give the command, give a quick jerk on the lead *after* you have given the command but do not repeat the command. You want him to come on one command only otherwise he will think the command is 'come, come, come.'

Most puppies have no problems with this exercise and will come very quickly and they will be leaping all over you with delight. This does not matter; it gives you a chance to praise your dog, for doing what you wanted, and to share in his joy. After a few seconds however you need to *take control* so stand in front of the dog, give him a 'sit' command, praise him for obeying, and then walk to the right of him and back into the heel position.

It is important that at this stage you always stand in front of the dog at the end of the exercise, before you return to the heel position because apart from the definition of 'come' meaning 'return to me as quickly as you can', the command will also start to mean 'face me' and the only way this will become clear to the dog is if the handler always ensures that these are the respective positions at the end of the exercise.

It is not necessary at this stage, for your dog to sit when he gets to you so do not try, too early to introduce this command.

I like to get the speed and joy aspects firmly in place for a young puppy first and they then seem to remember this as a pleasant experience all their life and that is exactly what I want, a dog which is happy to come back to me when commanded. I have found that to put a sit command in at the end of a recall, too early, starts to worry some puppies particularly the more sensitive ones. They want to come to me but seem to spend the whole journey worrying about doing the sit when they arrive, so they come slowly.

If you have any problem with this exercise it helps, with some puppies, if you crouch down, after you have given the command and the jerk on the lead. Do not bend down, as this is intimidating to some puppies, but simply kneel down on one or two knees but keep your back straight and in this way you are still in command but simply a little shorter!

Most puppies cannot resist coming immediately when they see you in this position so crouch down, let the puppy leap all over you with joy and be happy that he comes to you. Subsequently, once the puppy has learnt the meaning of the command, you can remain standing up.

As you progress with the exercise you can introduce a 'sit' command when he is almost back with you but to start, be happy with small miracles! The recall is an exercise where it is important for a handler to praise the dog for *starting* to obey a command, as this will be useful in the future. When the exercise is taught on the lead however, there is not enough time for most handlers to get the appropriate praise out after the initial 'come' command because the next second, the dog is leaping all over them.

It should not take long to progress with this exercise particularly if you have worked on the sit & walk round exercise off the lead, and are now able to walk a circle round your dog with ever increasing diameters. When progressing with the recall do not be tempted to do it off the lead until and unless your dog is coming to you with speed, instantly. After a few sessions, when your dog is responding immediately to the command on the lead, try the exercise by wrapping the lead round the dog's neck and tucking the end in so that he does not trip over it and finally, try it off the lead. Then you can build up some distance off the lead. It is important, when putting more distance between the dog and handler, prior to a recall command being given, that praise is given to the dog for getting up and *starting* to obey.

When introducing these progressions, do not over-face the dog by expecting the dog to remain steady whilst you go a vast distance away. There is no point! Keep the distance to a few paces only otherwise you risk the dog disobeying you when you are too far away to do anything about it. So remember this is training not *straining*! You should attempt at all times to ensure you do everything possible to enable the dog to obey and get it right.

It is at this stage, when a few paces away, when handlers should begin to praise the dog for *starting* to obey the command.

This is often a difficult period for young dogs because they are trying hard to remember everything they have been taught and most dogs do not want to go wrong. This is an excellent response from a dog because it means they are thinking but it may mean they are sometimes a little hesitant.

When you are doing a lot of steadiness type exercises and your dog is remaining in a sit position whilst different things are happening, when you actually *want* the dog to move, as on a recall, some dogs will hesitate, not sure if they are doing the correct thing.

This is what I would call a 'good fault', which sounds as though it is a contradiction of terms! The 'fault' part is that the dog is disobeying by hesitating but the 'good' bit indicates that the dog is thinking, being careful, working out in his own mind what he should do. This is an occasion where punishment, of any sort, is not needed and would in fact be counter-productive. This is because if the dog is thinking of whether he is going to do the correct thing by moving and a punishment was applied, the punishment would indicate to the dog that he was not right in his thinking. The dog would then be likely to sit down again or stay rooted to the spot.

If, on the other hand you praise the dog for his thinking 'am I right to move?' the praise will tell him, 'yes, you are doing the right thing'. I find it is often helpful to some puppies, to actually say 'yes', in an excited voice when I see the puppy working out what to do. This can often initiate the action of getting up. When the praise follows, the dog will speed up partly because he will then know his thinking is correct, but also because of the relief!

To see a dog responding in this way, tells me as an instructor, that the dog is learning rapidly and is trying to do his best to obey. If when given a recall command a dog gets up and starts to come towards you and you get a quick 'good boy' in, it speeds the dog up because the dog gains confidence in himself.

The sequence is therefore 'come', the dog thinks, handler says 'yes', so the dog starts to get up or move so the handler then says, 'good boy'. This then is followed by the dog continuing the action he thought was required, but was a little uncertain about, because he has also learnt that the 'good boy' means 'yes, you are doing the right thing'.

Some handlers get a little confused about this because they believe the dog should not be praised until the dog has finished the command given. Sometimes a dog may well have to continue with a command until a task is finished but that does not mean the dog cannot be praised whilst doing it. Praise really costs us humans very little but it is priceless to the dog! Praise will never stop a dog doing something and usually it encourages a dog to keep doing something and even to do it quicker!

Praise for initiating an action starts to enable a dog to understand that they must start to obey one command and will be praised for initiating the action but that sometimes they may be required to obey a subsequent command *before* they have completed the first command and sometimes *instead* of the first command. This may all sound a little complicated. It will all hopefully, become clear as you progress but at the moment just think of it as a reward to the dog for starting to obey. The reward will be sufficient to spur the dog on and enable him to obey the command with more speed, confident that he is doing it correctly simply due to the look on your face and the tone of your voice in praising him.

When building up the progressive stages from on the lead to off the lead and then putting a little more distance between yourself and the dog, if anything goes wrong, go back immediately to a previous stage which worked and keep on that stage for a few sessions before trying to progress. Don't ever let your dog do anything correctly or incorrectly without making the appropriate response of praising or a growl as necessary because this is how he will learn what is required and what you want him to do.

When you first start recall exercises it is tempting to try a recall in other circumstances such as in the house or when the dog is playing in the garden but it is much better not to give the command other than in a training session on formal exercises such as these. If you try recalling your dog in other circumstances and your dog takes no notice, you will teach him that sometimes he can disobey. He will learn this because you may have no way of enforcing the command so, until he has learnt the recall and you can combine a recall with other exercises, do not risk using the command at any other time.

Once your dog is coming to you on one command, with speed and delight, it will be time to put in a 'sit' command just before the dog gets all the way back to you. Most young puppies, at this stage have not learnt that they have 'brakes' and certainly have not learnt to use them. Bearing this in mind, and also going back to the personal space of the dog mentioned previously, it is no good for a handler to give the 'sit' command to the dog, when the dog is 6 inches away. The 'sit' command initially, should be given when the dog is *six feet* away from you. In that way you have, at least, some chance of getting the dog to sit, somewhere close to the desired position! If your dog does sit on command and ends up sitting several feet away from you, take that as a brilliant result! Just go to the dog, scratch him on the chest between the front legs, and praise him.

You will know that your dog obeys your commands instantly, and is also beginning to understand that he must obey the last command you give, even if he has not completed the action of a previous command. In subsequent sessions, you will be able to time the giving of the 'sit' command in accordance with where you want the dog to sit.

Progress on recalls should involve lengthening distances but you should always go back to your dog far more times than you ever call the dog to you. Practice can also involve other dogs and handlers with all the dogs sitting in a line and being recalled one at a time so that dogs become accustomed to responding to their own handler only. This is a vital part of your dog's education, and yours. If you were out on a shoot and recalled your dog, the last thing you want is for the other 6 dogs on the shoot to come to you too; neither do you want your dog going to anyone recalling their own dogs. Practice and experience is the only way your dog will learn these things.

When satisfactory progress has been made, a further enhancement can be added in giving your dog a verbal 'sit' command and later a stop whistle command when the dog is further away from you on recall. This should not be done too many times but it is a useful exercise to discover whether your dog is beginning to understand that he must obey the last command he is given rather than completing one command first.

Set a recall exercise up in the same way and decide, prior to giving the recall command, where you want your dog to stop and sit after the recall. This could be half-way between yourself and where you leave the dog in a sit, or anywhere at a distance away from you. The sequence then should be 'come, good boy, sit, good boy'. You should then go to the dog and praise him.

This ability to stop the dog a yard or many more away, following a recall command, will be used as the basis for more complex directional work later in the training programme, and will give you the valuable information that your dog is listening, is trying to obey you and is responding instantly to each command you give him even though he may not have completed a previous command.

Later, to test the recall command further you can combine some recall exercises with the quick sit exercises where you walk with the dog to heel, give a 'sit' command, and keep walking. These exercises were to test whether the dog understood the heel position but, as a variation to this, you could turn and face the dog and give a recall command, instead of a heel command.

It should always be remembered; whenever you are testing a dog's understanding of the recall and heel positions from a starting point at a distance from your dog, that whichever way you face, the dog should position himself appropriately.

Up to this point you have faced the dog before giving the recall command. This was to teach the dog that 'come', means return to me, but also means, *face me*. If the dog understands this, you should now be able to stand in any direction; sideways, facing him or with your back to the dog. When you give the recall command, the dog should return to you quickly and then position himself so that he faces you.

This is what tells you 'my dog understands the recall command, totally'.

Similarly when testing the heel command the command was taught in terms of a position (be on my left hand side, 6 inches away, with your right shoulder parallel with my left leg) but also came to mean *face in the same direction as me*. If the dog understands this, you should be able to move or stand in any direction; sideways, facing him or with your back to the dog. When you give the 'heel' command, when at a distance from the dog, he should return towards you and then position himself, so that he is facing in the same direction as you.

This is what tells you 'my dog understands the 'heel' command, totally'.

A note to end this section and that concerns the habit of some handlers who call their dog on their name when doing a recall. This is a bad habit to get into as dogs start to believe that their name means 'come'. Any name should merely alert a dog, or person, that someone has some kind of message for them. The name itself should not convey any kinds of message, other than, as far as gundogs are concerned, to go for a marked retrieve. That subject will be covered in a subsequent chapter but I put the note of caution here because it is on a recall that handlers frequently fall into the trap of using the name of their dog *instead* of a command word such as 'come'.

Now would be a good time to stop this habit, if by some chance you have allowed it to develop!

🐾 (t) Playing

Exploring and finding out about their new surroundings should be safe for a puppy and always supervised. A secure and fenced area should be provided whereby a puppy can explore.

(u)

Any play with older dogs should be controlled, supervised, and of short duration initially.

(Photographs: Paul Lawrence)

CHAPTER THIRTEEN

Going for walks and free play.

I believe that puppies, and older dogs just beginning training, should not be let off the lead in public places, however remote the place may appear. The only outdoor freedom a raw dog recruit should have is in your own secure garden or part of a garden which you have secured and made dog-proof and safe.

Dogs need exercise; young puppies need to develop physical skills, and all dogs need time to be dogs and maintain muscle development as well as develop and find meaning to messages received via their senses. Dogs need mental stimulation, need to be able think, reason, learn, and solve problems. They can do all of these things when involved in training sessions with you, periods of free play in a garden, playing and living in the home, and in periods of secure isolation in a kennel, car, cage or room in the house.

What they do not need, in my opinion, is for physical, emotional, and mental stimulation to be given free reign, and whilst all dogs need time to be alone and doing 'dog things' as opposed to dog/human things, this time should not be the whole or even the most of their day. Free play should never really be free. All activities should be supervised and an environment set up so that the dog is safe-guarded and wherever he is allowed to 'be a dog' has, as far as possible, been provided for him, rather than just happens to be there or somewhere 'we can take Fido to let off steam.'

Letting a dog off the lead in a situation which is not secure is the equivalent of letting a 3 year old child loose on a motorway; it is like getting into a car at the top of a hill, knowing the car has no brakes; it is like throwing an antique dinner service off a cliff.

Letting a dog off the lead, other than in very controlled circumstances is foolish, irresponsible and unfair. Teaching a dog to obey you; enabling a dog to develop his own sense of how to behave properly; being reasonably sure that you have the means to prevent the dog being a danger to other people, livestock, or to get into situations which will endanger him; all takes time but is an investment that must be made.

I find it astonishing that anyone can spend hundreds of pounds buying a new puppy and then believe that the only thing preventing them taking the puppy out for a walk off the lead is the fact that the puppy has not had its inoculations. As soon as this is achieved at approximately 12 weeks of age, many people then go out, let the dog off the lead, and before long, there is a problem. For most the problem is, 'my dog won't come back when I call him'! Of course he won't come back! Why should he? He has not been taught to come back!

The one thing which should prevent anyone taking a dog out and letting it free is that the dog has not yet been taught to obey the person who is with them, and until that happens the dog should not be allowed off the lead in any circumstances other that when a handler knows the dog is in a secure area at home. Otherwise the dog will be following his own programme of entertainment, and this generally will be concerning his senses and this will not include common sense!

You may think you are giving the dog physical exercise, a little run out, but the dog will not be thinking in terms of keeping himself fit but will be feeding his senses and reverting to instinctive behaviour which is based on finding, chasing, and devouring food! To a dog, scent is a drug and like a drug addict needing another fix, the more the dog gets, the more he wants, and he will eventually go to any lengths to get it. Yes, he will also be keeping himself physically fit but the fitter he gets in this way, the more unsound he will get in other ways, particularly when it comes to obeying people.

Gundogs bred for generations to be good game finders have their senses on full alert, but when very young they do not know fully what all the exciting smells and noises actually mean. To allow a dog to go off and investigate on his own, in circumstances when the handler has no means to prevent the dog doing this, will mean that the dog will learn, very rapidly, that he is free to please himself, can investigate anything which excites and interests him and most importantly, that his handler can do nothing about it.

To the dog, going for a walk off lead, is a hunting expedition. A handler should be master, should be leader of the pack and the dog should take second place on hunting expeditions. Frequently this develops into a reversal of the roles, the opposite of what is required for a good handler and dog partnership. A handler should not be frantically trying to keep up with the leading role adopted by the dog. Not only will the dog begin to believe he is in charge, because everyone is relying on him to find everything worthwhile, but he has actually been *given* this position from a very early age!

There will come a day when you will be able to take your dog out and let him off the lead for purposes other than walking to heel off lead, or any other reason attached to training, and this day will occur once the dog understands he must obey your commands, no matter what is happening around. A dog does not have to be fully trained but should, at the very least, understand the commands of 'heel', 'sit' and know what a recall means.

Due to the time that this takes, it will also mean that your dog is not only obedient to your commands, but he is learning to control himself. It is both of these factors which should govern the timing of allowing your dog freedom in unsecured areas. In this way, should the dog stray or be doing something you do not want him to do; you can give him an appropriate command, which he will obey. It also means that should the dog disappear from your sight, he will be starting, either to come back to you without being commanded on occasions he is uncertain, or will have begun to realise that some things happen in which he should take no part.

It is in the dog's interest not to stray too far from the pack! Whether the pack consists of only two; the leader and the dog, or numerous humans and/or other dogs then it is the responsibility of each dog to make sure he does not lose the leader of the pack.

It is not the responsibility of the leader to have to go round searching for the dog!

I accept that we must take responsibility for our dogs, and being a responsible owner always has to be in the back of our mind when we go out with dogs, but it is how an individual acts on this responsibility which should be the paramount consideration.

In my view, responsibility starts in giving a basic level of training to ensure a dog obeys commands most of the time. Ideally, obedience should be 100% *come what may*, but none of us can actually guarantee this. All we can do is make sure we have taught the dog, to the best of our ability and have been realistic in our assessment of the dog and ourselves in terms of whether the dog is, on the whole, obedient.

The next responsibility of the handler is to choose areas which are safe to go with a dog and this means safe from dangers *to* the dog due to hazardous terrain or proximity to roads and safe from dangers *from* the dog due to any livestock or natural vegetation.

You may think that there is very little to say about going out, letting the dog off the lead and simply enjoying the countryside. It is, after all, one of the reasons many people have a dog. A dog which is going to be, eventually, a working gundog is however a little different from a dog gained specifically as a pet companion, although whatever the eventual or hoped for role for the dog, it remains a fact that no dog should be let loose without the appropriate means to get it back or to save it or others, from any problems encountered.

Having ensured that all reasonable precautions have been taken regarding basic training then occasionally, go for a walk with your dog, either on your own, or in the company of others if you wish and enjoy it, but also allow the dog to enjoy it!

The problem people have when out for a walk, is constantly nagging the dog and this in turn creates problems for the dog. If you are out with your dog and have taken all the precautions as above then you should be able to relax without constantly worrying about him, calling him back to you, and giving every indication to the dog that you do not trust him. In this way the dog will also relax.

I repeat what I said earlier, *that it is the dog's responsibility to worry about us,* not the other way round. Otherwise the dog and not the handler is in the leadership position, and this in turn often encourages dogs to go further away, because they learn that they never have to ensure they do not lose the pack, and the pack leader, because the pack or the leader comes to look for them!

Calling a dog back to you constantly, or worrying all the time what the dog may be doing or where he is, gives the dog a false sense of security and is extremely unjust because you would be teaching the dog something which is not wanted or relevant to his position.

If a handler is constantly calling the dog back to them, this can also spell disaster because sooner or later the dog is going to get pretty fed up with it, and will start to disobey and eventually all you will be doing is teaching the dog, 'when we're out for a walk, I get anxious and will keep on nagging you and will worry about you all the time.'

As a result most dogs will eventually ignore you, mainly because you are acting in a way which does not make any sense to them. Depending on the nature of the dog he will either range further away and follow his own sources of amusement, ignoring any previously learnt commands, or with less bold dogs they will almost glue themselves to you thinking there must be something to worry about, therefore 'close ranks'. Neither of these is desirable.

Trust your dog, and trust your own belief that you have given the dog the training necessary. If you cannot trust yourself to behave appropriately, then do not take your dog out and let him off the lead.

When you go for a walk, later, when you *are* going to let the dog off the lead, put some control into the situation first by walking the dog to heel on the lead, for a short distance: sit the dog, walk away, return to the dog; sit the dog, and do a recall; any controlled exercise will do, to ensure you and the dog understand that this situation is not very different from all others up to this point. When you know you have control, you should then release the dog using your release command. I use 'OK, off you go', but hopefully you will have already chosen your own command for this.

Sometimes a dog does not understand what he should or is allowed to do at this point, so the best thing to do is encourage the dog but do not give him any commands, just let him find out that he is free to do what he wishes. If you have used your release command appropriately at home, such as when you return with the dog and you release him into the house or garden, he should be learning what this command means, and will now understand he is free here, in this place too. You can only put boundaries in later, if the circumstances warrant it. By this I mean just let your dog do and go where he wishes at this stage.

You should only call him back to you or give him some other command on the rare occasions when he may be about to do, or is doing, something you do not want him to do in which case, it would be an emergency situation.

Trust your dog to obey his natural pack instincts and let him worry, if necessary, about where you are and act appropriately to find you.

You can test these instincts, and I believe you should do this, by waiting until your dog is investigating something interesting and is at a distance from you, by hiding. Just hide behind a hedge, tree or turn on another path so you are out of sight of the dog. Then just stand and wait. Do not say anything or do anything. This is quite hard if you are of a nervous disposition or over anxious, but it will be well worth the effort! You will find that within a minute your dog will have found you! At this point just praise the dog. He has acted appropriately, not to a command you have given him, but in the interests of both you and himself, 'what a clever boy'!

After praising the dog give him the release command again. Usually at this point I say 'this way', which is not a command as much as an information statement which comes to mean, 'I am going this way now.' It does not mean 'you must come this way with me'. If this is what you want the dog to do, then the appropriate command would be 'heel', but this should not be necessary in these circumstances.

This small hiding exercise should give you a lot of satisfaction and confidence. You will know your dog is controlling himself, and your dog will know that the pack system he expects, is working well. Technically he did not lose the pack so much as the pack leader deliberately losing him, but it will have taught the dog a lot, particularly with regard to keeping half an eye, at least on what the leader is doing.

Try this exercise two or three times only. There is no point in setting this up more often but it is useful to try it again on a subsequent occasion when perhaps with other people and dogs.

I remember setting this exercise up one day with a training group. The whole group went for a walk on the local hills. There were approximately 12 people and about 15 dogs. Everyone had completed basic training and some had progressed further than this. All the dogs were let off the lead and were tearing round meeting and greeting all the dogs and people whilst we walked up a grassy track.

When all the dogs were ahead of us, the people part of the pack turned off the track and hid amongst a group of trees. We just stood there in silence. It took about 5 seconds for the first dog to find us and within 30 seconds the whole group of dogs was back with us.

The other remarkable thing was that, on this occasion, because the people part of the pack were simply standing, doing nothing, by the time all the dogs joined us they too did nothing. There were 12 people and 15 dogs standing in a group, doing nothing. The dogs were controlling themselves, not necessarily standing with their handlers but just waiting for the pack to decide what should happen next. Perfect pack behaviour! No commands had been given to the dogs but there was a look of total shock on the faces of some of the handlers!

I know many people in the group were amazed at this, some having said before hand 'oh, I don't think I'd better do this, my dog runs off and no matter how much I call him, he won't come back for ages'. Most of the people part of the pack had not understood this need in the dog to remain with the pack. They had seen their role as one of looking after the dog.

Most of the time with dogs, we are teaching them our rules, our way of how they should behave, *but* we must make use of the dog's pack instincts too, especially the ones which fit in with our society and the ones which we want to develop for our benefit. Keeping up with the pack, not getting lost and being there in the midst of the pack makes total sense to a dog and all the dogs, on this occasion reverted to their known pack instincts and, from the view-point of the handlers, were totally controlled.

☙ (v) The 'get over' command

Puppies beginning to learn the meaning of the 'get over' command, by using a small plank across a gateway in the process of doing some heelwork.

(Photographs: Mary Ward)

CHAPTER FOURTEEN

The 'get over' command.

The definition of the 'get over' command to the dog is: negotiate and/or get to the other side of any obstacle in front of you, going away from me.

These are the command words I use. You will need to choose your own command word or words and then stick to it, or them, for life. I shall use the words 'get over' throughout.

Many things will be seen as an obstacle to a dog and a handler needs to recognize that, although from a handler's point of view, something like an open fence with a clear view through to the other side seems easy enough to get through, from a dog's point of view it may as well be a brick wall.

The command does not mean *jump*, although this is one action which could be required and it is important that handlers do not begin to believe that the command word means anything other than the definition otherwise you may start introducing a variety of commands for different obstacles, none of which, I believe, are necessary. The one term covers *any* obstacle.

Anything in front of the dog, which is different from the terrain he is currently running over, is a potential obstacle. This means therefore that a pathway crossing a field can be seen as an obstacle to the dog and many dogs would not want to cross it. Added to this are the following: a stream, ditch, river, lake, wall, fence, hedge, track or anything, over or through which a dog must pass, when given the command.

The best way to teach the 'get over' command at the beginning is by using a small jump. You can create one for yourself if necessary by putting a broom across two chairs, a plank across a gateway or a slim box in a doorway. Whatever you construct needs to be wide enough and fairly low so you can get across it with your dog on a lead. You can use a purpose-built jump for dogs or horses or use anything which is either already in existence or easy to construct and over which you can get too!

This command can be introduced at any time during the process of heelwork exercises and the idea is not to teach the dog to jump any great height at this stage, but simply for the dog to begin to understand the meaning of the word and to experience at least one of the situations in which it will apply.

Handlers need to be careful with young puppies, not to expect them to jump anything other than a fairly low height, in relation to the dog's size and have regard to the growing joints and bones to ensure puppies do not injure themselves or damage the soft, growing areas of joints, particularly hips, elbows and shoulders.

At this stage one is merely introducing the dog to the command and later developments with this command can introduce more height as well as different types of obstacles found naturally in the countryside where you will be training.

Training.

It is necessary here to remember again, the 6 foot area of a dog's *personal space* mentioned in numerous situations before and remember too that the command is to mean 'negotiate any obstacle *in front.*'

Stand a few paces away from the jump with your dog on the lead. The jump should therefore be within 6 feet of you. Say 'heel' and then immediately say 'get over'. Walk forward with the dog at heel and step over the jump. Hopefully the dog will simply step over the jump with you and you can then praise him and keep walking. This does not mean that the dog now understands the command but if you do it a few times you will begin to see whether the dog has grasped the principle.

Provided the dog has not shown any sign of being worried after doing it a few times you can take this a little further. Say 'heel' and walk towards the jump as before. Say 'get over', but just hang back for a second or two. Most dogs will get over the jump and you can remain on the first side without going over yourself until after the dog has jumped at which point you can step over too. That will tell you that the dog is beginning to understand. If the dog does not get over the jump continue with stepping over yourself and then try again next session.

In subsequent heelwork sessions you can develop this a little further by having different types of small obstacles to negotiate in the process of walking round with your dog on and off the lead. You can also try a recall across the jump in the following way: leave the dog in a sit while you step over and go to the other side of the jump. Keep the lead on the dog, in the same way as you practiced when first starting to teach the dog the recall command of 'come', and then recall the dog over the jump using a verbal or whistle command.

If this goes well, you can then try the same exercise off the lead but this should only be tried if you have a small barrier across a gateway or similar so that the dog cannot just go round the barrier.

When doing the jump in a recall direction it is important not to use the 'get over' command but just use the recall. The reason for this is that the meaning of 'get over' needs to begin to mean an obstacle *in front,* but also mean *going away from me* and although the obstacle is technically in front of the dog when you are teaching in this way, it is not going away from you, it is coming towards you. Later the obstacles will always be in front when the dog is going away from you. If you teach the dog now that 'get over' can mean going away from you *and* coming back to you, you will have problems!

Training therefore needs to include the 'get over' command *only* when the dog is going away from you.

You do not need to do a great deal more at this stage but when developing work on other exercises such as recalls and later, simple marked retrieves, you may find natural obstacles which can be incorporated: for example, recalls across small ditches, marks into cover over banks, or through a hedge.

Remember that when a dog is returning to you the command is a recall and not a 'get over'. You need to be consistent in this and then the dog will understand you mean an obstacle in front of him, going away from you. Some people do not understand why this is necessary so I will explain.

The reason is as follows: suppose you want your dog to go across a field, jump a fence, take a right turn and then go cross a lake. You would have to send your dog across the field and say 'get over' when he gets to the fence. When he has jumped the fence you would need to stop him and then send him to the right at which point you would have to say 'get over' again – to mean get over the lake, which would then be the next obstacle in front of him going away from you.

If you train your dog to believe 'get over' can mean when he is going away from you *and* when he is coming back towards you, in this situation he would immediately jump back across the fence he has just jumped, which is not what you want. A dog must be trained to believe that 'get over' only means in front of him, going away from the handler, and he will know therefore that he has to turn immediately and look for something else to get over in front of him, further away. He therefore will not turn to get back over the jump and start coming towards you.

Use whatever you can find in training to further your dog's experience of all manner of obstacles so that everything he is likely to meet, he has already seen and dealt with.

I once had a puppy which, when competing in a puppy gundog working test, was expected to get over an orange fertilizer bag which had been tied up over a gap in a fence. She had never seen one of these in her life, and to make matters worse, there was a strong wind and the bag was blowing about as well as sounding very strange with crackling noises and a sort of roaring as the wind went through the bag. My puppy watched the dummy being thrown, wanted to go and get it but no way was she going to jump the orange monster lurking in the bushes and roaring!

I now try to introduce puppies to fertilizer bags of all hues and cries!

Obstacles can easily be assembled at home for puppies, to give them experience at an early age, for almost everything they are likely to encounter in life. Most people have, in their garden shed, everything needed. These obstacles do not have to be vast edifices because remember you are not teaching the puppy to jump a great height or solve Mensa type problems, but simply enabling the puppy to see and experience, what to him, is strange.

A small length of pig or chicken wire netting, fertilizer bag, a piece of trellis or fencing can all be attached between two canes; a pole with a gap underneath can be put between two chairs. Anything you can find will be excellent experience provided it is safe, not too high and cannot collapse and frighten the puppy.

Out in the countryside, use as many natural features as you can find such as, ditches, streams, tracks, banks and hedges. Aim to give the puppy the opportunity to have a small amount of experience on all these things when he is young, and he will begin to understand the 'get over' command in all its many guises and will in fact begin to look for something when you give the command.

☙ (w) Teaching a dog to hold items of your choosing

(Left) Hold the item in front of the dog and give the 'hold' command or gently place the item in the dog's mouth and say 'hold'

(Right) Praise the dog and scratch her on the chest between the front legs as this will normally cause the dog to lift her head up.

(x)

(Above) Some dogs want to put the dummy in *your* mouth! It doesn't matter, just keep praising and let the dog enjoy it. You should then *take control* put the dog on a sit, take hold of the item and give the release command 'give' or 'dead'.

(Photographs: Paul Rawlings)

CHAPTER FIFTEEN

Developing work on the 'hold' and 'give' commands.

During your progress with teaching your dog the commands so far and the variety of exercises to help the dog to understand these commands in differing situations and circumstances you will, hopefully have also spent some time teaching him the 'hold' and 'give' commands away from formal training sessions.

It is time now to incorporate this into your training sessions.

Your dog should be at the stage, whereby he will take any item from your hand, when you say 'hold'. After you have praised him and taken hold of the item yourself, your dog should then be releasing the item when you say 'give'. You will not, up to this stage have thrown anything for your dog and hopefully, you will not have allowed anyone else to throw anything for your dog either!

Many young dogs have an item which they favour so on your next training session, take the favourite item with you but put it in your pocket or game bag. It does not matter what the item is but it should be something which you have used on special occasions when you and your dog have been involved in this special 'hold and give' game he is allowed to play with you.

Do some of your normal training exercises and when in the process of doing some heel work, get your 'hold' item out of your bag and as you are walking along, put the item in front of the dog and say 'hold'. The dog should know what to do and will take hold of the item and walk along in the heel position holding his special item. Do not try to walk very far. Take a few paces reminding the dog 'heel' as well as 'hold' and then halt and give the dog a 'sit good boy, hold good boy'. You should then stand in front of the dog, remind him 'hold, good boy' scratch his chest between his front legs and then take the item from the dog with a 'give, good boy'. Then repeat the 'sit, good boy' and, walking to the right of your dog, move round the back of him and back into the correct heel position. You can then put the lead back on or do some further exercises without the lead, keeping your dog under perfect control throughout.

If you think back to the section earlier in this book on presenting, you will appreciate that your dog, at this stage has just achieved a perfect present:

- He was sitting in front of you.
- He was holding an item in his mouth.
- He was holding his head up.
- He waited until you had hold of the item.
- When you said 'give' he released the item.
- He remained in a sit position, off lead, whilst you walked round him and back into the heel position.

If all goes well, do not try this again until your next training session, when things can be taken a little further. If there are any problems it should be immediately evident where you will need to do some more work, either in terms of heelwork, sit, steadiness or continuing with the 'hold' and/or 'give' training elsewhere. Correct any difficulties appropriately before trying this exercise again in a few days or weeks.

Some of you may be getting impatient and wondering 'when is my dog going to start retrieving?' Your patience is soon to be rewarded!

Retrieving.

Retrieving is a very interesting, and complex subject and yet many people would suggest that there is very little of true interest or complexity in the act of fetching something although many would perhaps agree that it is the *way* that this is done which adds a little interest and some retrieves, *per se* may well be more complicated than others.

If, however, *a retrieve* is broken down into its component parts it becomes truly remarkable. For a start, in gundog speak, the word retrieve is used predominantly as a noun and although I am sure someone will say I am wrong in this, I have never known the word to be used in this way in normal language or any other activity.

The word is normally a verb 'to retrieve' and is to do with the act of fetching. In gundog circles however it is used frequently as a noun as well as a verb, and as such does not mean only the act of fetching but includes the item fetched as well as how it is done.

It is common for retrieves to be spoken of, requested, commented on and described in detail concerning; marked, seen, blind, unseen, puppy retrieves, novice retrieves, open retrieves, poor retrieves, wonderful retrieves, retrieves in the open, retrieves in woodland, water retrieves, and retrieves from over obstacles.

Handlers get personally attached to these things called retrieves and say such things as 'my retrieve', or 'his retrieve was easier than mine' or 'can I have another retrieve?'

A retrieve can also mean the item involved such as a dummy, a ball, a game bird or anything really, and one hears such things as 'I will put you out a retrieve', but it is not the act of retrieving these things which is referred to as the retrieve, but the item itself.

All these terms have a special meaning to those who know! It is all part of the jargon of the gundog world and will make little sense to those not connected but will hopefully begin to make some sense to those who wish to become connected!

So what is a retrieve?

I believe the verb to retrieve in gundog terms is 'to hold'. To retrieve is simply what occurs in that second or two when a dog opens his mouth, picks up an item and holds it.

To retrieve is therefore to hold.

Of course there are many more complicated definitions given by gundog trainers instructors and handlers and if they are asked to describe a retrieve, many will go into all types of explanation concerning the dog's steadiness, going on command, answering all manner of subsequent commands to cover distances over grassland, through woods, over lakes and fences, going left, going right, searching for the item and then returning to the handler.

These are all vital aspects of a dog's training, all crucial, and necessary and without all this the dog would not be able to retrieve satisfactorily but I believe most of these to be the journey, out and back, which enables the retrieve to take place.

Many people fail to include in this description a section which involves this crucial act of taking into the mouth the required item and in so doing fail also to teach the dog a command word for this major act.

This in turn means that they in fact leave this aspect to the dog to decide whether he picks the item up or not. Most dogs will pick up items but what happens when a dog does not or will not pick up an item? What can the handler do in these circumstances?

The handler has nothing to use, no tool in the form of a taught and learnt command at his disposal, to use either to help the dog, or to get the dog to bring the item back to the handler.

How a dog performs on all aspects of the journey out and back is an important consideration, but eventually the best performance in the world is not going to compensate for not retrieving the bird.

Of course retrieve to most people means fetch – you go away, get something and bring it back but when it comes to teaching a dog all the separate parts of this it is important, I believe, to concentrate on my preferred definition of retrieve meaning hold.

Training.

Most of the hard work regarding teaching your dog to retrieve will already have been done by the time you get to this stage of your training, although the journey part of retrieving has yet to be learnt.

In case anyone thinks *'we are doing all this the wrong way round'*, I perhaps need to explain my philosophy concerning this aspect of training. Many people start a gundog's training by throwing countless items for the dog to chase and pick up. This was the way retrieving was traditionally taught and was the way I was encouraged to train my dogs in the past. What I found, and failed to find satisfactory answers for, was the problem of dogs willing to run-in, quite happy to chase, thrilled to pick something up *BUT:* very reluctant to return to me with the item picked up; or would come back half-way, then run off; or would come back and drop the item; or would hunt and find the item but not pick it up because the dog enjoyed hunting for it only and lost interest once it was found.

I now teach dogs, and teach other people, that retrieves should be taught from the hold and present backwards. This is called reverse chaining and means that dogs are not encouraged to run after anything in the beginning, and are taught control aspects first.

Handlers should take control of all these aspects because they have little chance of taking control of a dog that is 2 fields away and doing what he likes, particularly when the dog has learnt few, if any, commands.

Thus far then, you and the dog have learnt several control factors relating to retrieving in that the dog is steady, and knows how to take something into his mouth and release it to you on command. You have taught the dog to walk to heel on and off the lead, a recall and your dog will walk off lead holding an item of your choice and he will present it to you correctly.

Having successfully managed to get your dog to hold and walk to heel followed by a good present, it will be time to go a little further.

You have now gathered all the ingredients together, so it is now time to blend them together!

The next progression is as follows:

- On your next training session take a hold item with you in your pocket or game bag as before. Do a little heelwork or other exercises to establish control and settle the dog down into work mode. Put your dog on a sit, off lead, and do a sit & walk round and walk through the heel position in the same way as if you were going to do a re-call or calling the dog into the heel position. This is all work which your dog knows. Face your dog and remind him with 2 or 3 'sit, good boy' commands and then return to the dog, to the right, round the back and back into the heel position.
- Then stand in front of the dog, put your hold item in front of the dog and give him the 'hold' command. The dog should take the item from you. Remind him 'sit, hold good boy' and then walk round him and through the heel position and take up the recall position, facing the dog a few paces away. Remind the dog 2 or 3 times, 'sit, good boy' then say 'come'. The only thing which is different for the dog is the fact that he is holding something, but everything else should be the same. Your dog should start moving as soon as he hears the 'come' command, at which point you can praise him. As he gets towards you remind him 'hold, good boy', crouch down and praise the dog. After praising the dog, command him 'sit, hold, good boy' and stand up, repeating the commands as necessary. Scratch the dog on the chest and then hold onto the item and give the release command. It is important at this

stage to keep control of the dog so remind him sit, whilst you put the hold item away and then walk to the right of the dog, round the back and return to the heel position. You should then put the lead on the dog or do a few heelwork exercises before finishing. Do not do another hold exercise that session.

If all went well, you can be very pleased with yourself and the dog. The dog has now successfully achieved most of the requirements for a retrieve but more importantly, you the handler have *taken control* of all aspects from start to finish.

On subsequent training sessions, this can be taken further but do not do too much; one or two hold type exercises each session is sufficient and most work should be on the heelwork, recall, leave-it and steadiness exercises already learnt.

If anything goes wrong, it should be clear to you, where more work needs to be done and this exercise should not be attempted again until any area of difficult has been corrected. This could be steadiness or recalls, which should be corrected with no 'hold' involved, or if the area of difficulty was concerning the hold or release, correct these separately and go back to practising away from formal training sessions.

Progression should then be as follows:

- With the dog in the heel position, step forward, leaving the dog on a sit, and place your hold item on the ground, a pace or two in front of the dog. Now is the time to begin introducing the dog to a slightly new command and that is to go on their name. Step back into the heel position and then give the dog the 'hold' command but prefix this with the dog's name. So the command will be 'Brave (or whatever the dog's name is) Hold'. Hopefully your dog will pick the item up and you can then give him the recall command. Remember to keep control of all parts, particularly the return to you. The dog will require lots of praise but then you gain control by putting the dog on a sit and follow the same routine of going round the dog. These taught and learnt aspects should never change at this stage as they give the dog confidence in the things they know and enable the dog to accept the small new bits to each exercise.

- Start increasing the distance when you walk away from the dog and place the hold item on the ground. Do not throw the item but simply do the same exercise varying the distance until the dog will leave your side on his name and the 'hold' command. Once the dog is doing this, you can stop giving the 'hold' command, and simply send the dog on his name only. The dog will never forget what 'hold' means, but this was simply a teaching tool and will only be used in future if your dog is uncertain about whether to pick something or not and can then be used to encourage him in terms of reassuring him that, 'yes, that's what I want you to retrieve'.

CHAPTER SIXTEEN

The Whistle

The use of a whistle to give a variety of commands to a gundog is for several reasons:

- Gundogs are possibly the only group of dogs which, when working, are having to work sometimes at quite a distance from their handlers.
- They work predominantly in the winter months when weather conditions are arguably at their worst.
- These two facts mean that verbal commands may be difficult for a dog to hear when at a distance or gale force winds and rain may be taking sound away from the dog rather towards it.
- Whistle sounds carry far more effectively in wintry conditions and unlike human voices, the whistle does not get hoarse and tired by the end of the day, and stays true to pitch under all circumstances (other than when it gets clogged with mud!).
- Gundog handlers on a shoot also have to be aware that they are very much the backstage help! The guns are the people who are paying for the day and they do not want constant voices bellowing out commands to dogs.
- Birds too can be affected by the noise of humans and we have to be careful to keep noise to a minimum when working in close proximity to game birds, being careful particularly not to disturb too many which may be required for subsequent drives during the day.

So, the use of a whistle is much less intrusive to others on the shoot, as well as being a more effective tool in terms or conveying our wishes to a dog at distance.

There is a limit to how many different commands can be taught for the whistle but these are generally those for a 'sit' or stop, a recall and some people use a whistle command as a 'hie lost' hunting command.

Whistles should, as with other commands, be used sparingly so that the commands have some impact, and so that dogs do not learn to ignore a whistle. You should consider carefully what type of whistle to buy or seek advice from an instructor if uncertain. Most people opt for a plastic whistle of either 210½ pitch or 211½ pitch. Plastic whistles are also available with a pea inside. This gives a warbling sound effect and the whistles are also slightly louder. All these whistles remain true to pitch and whenever you buy a replacement it will always sound the same as the previous one.

The so-called 'silent' whistles are not normally used by gundog handlers. Some people buy stag horn whistles, which look very good but I have never favoured them due to the fact that they are all of slightly different pitch and an identical one can never be purchased when a replacement is needed.

In addition to a whistle, you will also need to purchase a lanyard. This is simply a cord, of some material, to which you attach the whistle and hang round your neck. They range from simple string types to expensive, plaited leather and the choice is simply one of personal preference. Essentially, the lanyard keeps your whistle safe until you want to use it and you should not try and use a whistle without some kind of attachment of it, to you.

I think it is important to understand that the whistle itself has no magical properties! The use of a whistle command has to be taught to the dog, the same as the use of a verbal command or a hand signal command. This may seem a concept which is not worth mentioning but you would be surprised at the number of people who have told me such things as: 'Oh, I did buy a whistle once but I blew it and the dog didn't come back, so I never used it again!' 'I bought a whistle but it didn't work, the dog took no notice. What sort have you got? Do you think if I got one of those, it would work better?'

It is difficult to know where to start, when faced with such comments and questions, so I tend not to!

When going to choose a whistle however, it is important to try it and blow it softly as well as loudly and see which suits you best and what you feel comfortable with; then teach the dog what each command means, carefully and systematically.

I use the following whistle commands:

- 1 short toot to mean 'sit'. This later becomes a stop command when the dog is working at a distance but is taught to mean 'sit' at the beginning. Later it begins to mean stop, and more importantly 'watch me, because I am going to give you another command and/or help you.
- Several short, rapid toots to mean 'come'. For this command I use 3 rapid toots, immediately followed by another three. This means come back to me quickly. You must decide for yourself, how many toots you give, and then stick to this throughout the dog's life.
- Several short, slow toots to mean come towards me. Many people use a similar command as a hunting command, to mean 'hie lost'. It cannot be used for both, so you need to make the decision. My 'come towards me' consists of 2 slow toots, a slight pause, followed by another 2 slow toots.

The first command you should teach the dog is the 'sit', one toot command and to begin the whistle command training, the dog needs to know the verbal command of 'Sit', to which he responds quickly and consistently to the first and only command given.

It is important to keep your whistle in your mouth and learn how to talk as well as keep your whistle in position. Most people do this by holding the whistle in their teeth thus allowing speech without the whistle slipping out of the mouth. It takes practice however!

Start by using the whistle in heel work and start with heel work on the lead. Say 'heel' and walk a few paces and then stop. Say 'sit' and then give the whistle command. If you have taught your dog to sit immediately the verbal command is given, it will be in the process of sitting when you give the whistle command. Practice for a while giving both verbal and whistle commands and prompt verbal praise each time. After a while, you can stop giving the verbal command and use the whistle command only.

In the same way as the verbal command was taught, it is important to give only one whistle command and make the dog respond to that command. It is also important to make sure you are not blowing the whistle too vigorously. When your dog is at heel, very little volume should be used. Save your mightiest blow for when the dog is ½ a mile away. Many handlers behave at this stage as though their dog is deaf or as if the sheer force of the blow will stop the dog and make him sit!

If you have been putting in a hand signal to sit, when leaving the dog or practicing recalls you will find with practice, that eventually the dog will sit when given any of the commands of verbal, whistle or hand signal to sit. You will need to try it out several times and make sure your dog understands. When you are confidant that your dog will respond to all the individual commands; the verbal command of 'sit', a whistle command to sit and the hand signal, then you can begin the whole sequence again off the lead.

It is better to start at the beginning again when the dog is off the lead so begin with the verbal and whistle and then progress from there. Whenever you stop and give a sit command, it is very important that you remember to give the dog a 'heel' command when you start walking again if you expect the dog to come with you. It is in this way that you will teach the dog that he must obey the last command you gave and continue obeying that command until you give another command.

If you have told a dog to sit, then that is what he must do no matter what is happening around him and no matter what you do. If you are consistent, each stage of training will be a natural progression and you will not be trying to undo faults which you have caused or created.

The next whistle command you can teach is the recall command which is your choice of several short, rapid toots. The number of toots used is a matter of personal preference but needs to be 2 or more toots in quick succession.

I have 2 recall commands; for the first I use 3 short toots followed by another 3 toots. This means to the dog, 'return to me as quickly as possible'. You need to decide how many toots and *how* you will whistle and then stick to it for ever.

To teach the dog the meaning of the recall whistle the dog needs first of all to know the verbal command of 'come' or whatever command you have chosen, (other than its name!)

The dog needs to be at the stage of coming to you immediately the command is given and responding to the first and only command you give. Having taught a recall to the dog on the lead it is important to wait whilst any heelwork difficulties are sorted out and your dog is responding to 'heel' commands and 'sit' commands. Unless a dog can sit in one place and remain sitting until you give further commands there is no point in trying to teach a recall off the lead.

To teach a whistle recall you need first of all to ensure your dog will do the following; walk to heel off and on the lead, sit on a verbal, whistle or hand signal and will stay in a sit position whilst you walk away and return to the dog. As with each new command we teach the dog, it is important to go back to a stage the dog already knows and then start adding new bits. Your dog already knows how to do a recall on the lead and what the word 'come' means so that is the point to start. Have the dog on a lead and follow the procedure for a recall learnt so far. When you turn to face the dog, have your whistle in your mouth, say 'come' and immediately follow this with your whistle command. Practice several times over a few days or weeks and then you should not need to use the verbal command very often although it is a good plan to use it now and again just to ensure that the dog understands that obedience to the command applies, however the command is given.

Once the dog is coming immediately on a whistle command you can begin the whole process again off the lead. When you try off the lead, try to stay fairly close to begin. Go back to your basic recall procedure and use the verbal command followed by the whistle. Once the dog is responding instantly to a whistle recall off the lead start increasing the distance you move away from the dog and then you can drop the verbal 'come' command and just use the whistle command.

You should not recall your dog every time you move away from him. You do not want the dog to start thinking that every time you face him you are going to recall him. It is important to vary what you do, once you know a dog has learnt a particular command, and you should therefore return to your dog as often, if not more, than you recall him.

Although the dog may well be responding well to whistle commands, these should never be seen as a total substitute for verbal commands. The whistle should be used sparingly and it is important that you continue to use verbal commands on occasions too so the dog does not start to think along the lines of, 'well, I didn't hear the whistle, so I'm not going to sit'. All the commands you use have to be obeyed. You are the leader and whether you decide to use voice, whistle or hand signal is irrelevant to the dog in terms of whether he obeys or not. He must obey, no matter what!

It is tempting, once you have taught the dog about the recall whistle, to use it in other circumstances. It is much better, at this stage not to do this in any situation apart from in a formal training session. The reason for this is that you may be tempted to use the recall when you have absolutely no chance of making the dog obey the command, such as when he is in the garden, you want to go out and you should have left home 10 minutes ago! In these circumstances your dog knows you are going out, believe me! A recall may be tempting but many dogs are going to ignore it! Why? Because the master is going out, the dog thinks or knows he will not be going too; hence 'I'm going to play up and not go in!'

You should find another method for getting over this type of situation (bribery comes to mind, if all else fails!) and it is much better not to risk any of your commands in a situation you may not win. You must win every time you give a command which means every command you give must be obeyed. If you cannot ensure this happens, the *only* thing you can do is not give the command. It also means you should think before you act. It is no good giving a command, your dog ignoring it and then you thinking, 'perhaps I should not have given the command'. You are then into trying somehow to make the dog obey and often dogs will win these encounters as they are much more proficient in strategies!

Flow chart (3) – for the latter stages of training.

- H/W and steadiness training off lead. The whistle to be used for 'sit' and recall commands.
- The dog understands and obeys controlled access to car and control at doors/gateways.
- The dog is steady off lead to thrown dummies and other dogs working.

↓

- Teach a marked retrieve.
- Develop work near and into water.

↓

- Practice all exercises in different places amongst other handlers and dogs. Progress with marked retrieves.

↓

- Teach the 'get-on' command.
- Teach the 'go back' command.
- Develop the go back in other places and start to involve other dogs and handlers.

↓

- Vary distances for marked retrieves as well as varying types of terrain.
- Continue heelwork off lead and include walking in line with others with about turns. Develop whistle work to include sit at a distance on recall and for present on a retrieve.

↓

- Teach the dog about blind retrieves which is a development of the 'go back' command. Develop blinds as part of normal training sessions and include working in different places.

↓

- Develop directional work to include combination commands, on retrieves, of 'go back' and 'get on' with occasional recalls.

↓

Check list.
1. Dog is steady under all circumstances.
2. Dog understands whistle commands for recall and sit.
3. Dog able to do a marked retrieve on 'name' command.
4. Dog understands and obeys directional commands of 'go back' and 'get on'.

CHAPTER SEVENTEEN

A Marked retrieve

A 'Mark' is a simple retrieve whereby the dog and handler see a dummy thrown and see where it lands. It is sometimes called a 'seen' retrieve because of this. Whichever term you use the throwing of the dummy should be accompanied, certainly in these early stages, by the word, 'Mark', said by whoever is throwing the dummy. Later a dummy may simply be thrown, on occasions, without the word being said, or there may be a gun-shot as the dummy is thrown.

The command for sending a dog to retrieve a marked dummy is the dog's name. It is the only occasion where you should use your dog's name and most gundog handlers use this method to send the dog because it is quick, efficient and usually unique in that mostly, other dogs are not called the same. If you are standing in line with other handlers and dogs, all dogs are off lead and all dogs have been taught to go on the same command, chaos reigns! For example, suppose everyone taught their dog to retrieve a mark on the command 'fetch'. What would happen, in the excitement of the moment, is that one handler would say 'fetch' and probably the dogs on either side would go too and possibly all the dogs in line! It is for this reason that handlers now use their dog's name for this type of retrieve.

If you choose to use some other command for a marked retrieve, that is up to you but *you have been warned!*

To begin a marked retrieve your dog needs to be steady that means he should sit when you give him the command, and should stay in a sit position whilst you walk away and return. He should understand a recall and will have practiced 'hold' and 'give' whilst sitting and on a recall. You should also be at the stage where your dog has learnt to leave your side after you have put a dummy or other item, on the ground and he will hold the item and come back to you. When practicing the above you should have started to omit the 'hold' command when sending your dog and he should be going on his name command only.

You are aiming at the situation whereby you and the dog see a marked retrieve, you say the dogs name and the dog goes to fetch the dummy. No other words or actions are necessary from the handler so you must try not to use your hands, not to say anything and do not step forward. It is also important that whoever is throwing the mark says 'mark' only once before throwing the dummy.

Training.

As with most other exercises, the progress towards this final stage for retrieving a marked dummy will be done gradually but usually, this is fairly swift progress.

To begin: Start with some heelwork, and other steadiness exercises already learnt and then go on to the exercise last attempted when furthering your work on the hold command, when you walked out and placed a dummy on the ground a few paces from the dog. When you place the dummy on the ground say 'mark'. Everything else should remain the same, so return round the back of your dog and into the heel position. Then say your dog's name, with a 'hold' if your dog is not yet going on his name alone. Your dog should go forward, pick up the dummy and then return to you. This means everything is the same as he has already achieved and the only new bit was when you said 'mark' when placing the dummy.

If your dog does not do this perfectly, you will need to correct any areas where there was a perceived difficulty, and wait for a few days before attempting the marked retrieve training again.

If all goes well however, it will be time to take things a little further. Stand in the heel position with your dog off the lead on a sit. Remind your dog 'sit, good boy' and then throw a dummy a few yards forward saying 'mark' as you throw it. Make sure you keep your eyes on your dog, whilst you are doing this, and do not watch the dummy. Remind the dog 'sit, good boy' wait a second or two and then say the dogs' name.

Hopefully the dog will leave your side, pick up the dummy and return to you because most of this is what he already knows and if everything is satisfactory try the same thing once more. Next, instead of sending the dog, do everything the same, but remind your dog 'sit, good boy', leave the dog there and you go and pick up the dummy. Then do no more that session. You must not begin inadvertently to teach your dog that every time he hears the word 'mark' that he is going to retrieve whatever has been thrown, so take control and keep control!

Most people do not have any problems with this stage but inevitably, with some dogs, there may be problems.

If your dog does not leave your side, try and encourage him. He may not be at all certain what he has to do, so if necessary step forward with him, or go all the way with him if you need to and when you get to the dummy, say 'hold'. It is difficult to say precisely what you should do because all dogs have different reactions to this. After spending so much time on steadiness exercises, throwing dummies when the dog was not allowed to move, many dogs almost think this is some kind of trick. They will soon get over it and it is far more preferable to have a dog which thinks about things and remains in a sit rather than doing the wrong thing, than a dog which goes charging off and does the wrong thing in a more spectacular manner! So help the dog as much as you can whilst keeping everything possible the same as he has already learnt. Try not to use punishment for a dog which may be a little cautious. You need to lighten the proceedings so be silly, run out with the dog, make it fun and encourage rather than discourage and go over the top with praise one the dog understands.

Try this 2 or 3 times, encouraging all the time, if necessary, and then do no more. Let the dog think about it for a day or two and you will find the dog will probably do it correctly and with enthusiasm on the next training session.

Before progressing further, your dog should be able to go for a marked retrieve, a few yards away, on his name and with no movement from you, the handler. The dog should also be picking up the dummy and returning to the handler and presenting the dummy appropriately. If some of this is not happening, do not progress further but put right any areas of difficulty first. If you allow any sloppiness in retrieving at this stage, it will only get worse as you progress so it is well worth spending extra days or weeks in practicing and correcting any areas which are not quite right, and getting them correct before moving on.

Progressing with marked retrieves.

It is at this stage you should aim to get someone else involved who can throw a dummy for you and you should be careful not to throw dummies yourself.

Many people find this difficult when training, partly because handlers are desperate to begin, what they think of as 'proper retrieving' and the handlers continue to say 'mark' and throw dummies as far as they can. The main problem with this is that you will already have taught and encouraged your dog to look at you when you give a command, or praise, or say anything. This is good but when it comes to retrieving a mark, what is required is that the dog should keep looking ahead, looking for the mark to see where it lands.

Often dogs are described as 'poor markers' in that when sent on command, the dog does not go immediately to the fall, where the dummy landed, but is hunting either all the way out, or in the wrong place when they have gone out. Sometimes this is a difficulty one or two individual dogs have, but most often, a handler has created these problems for the dog either by throwing too many dummies themselves or when someone else throws the dummy, the *handler* says 'mark'. Many dogs in these circumstances look at their handler and therefore do not look at the most important person saying 'mark', which is the dummy thrower, and consequently see neither the dummy being thrown nor the fall, hence the 'poor marking'.

To get over this some handlers will then do the following: walk out in front of the dog, say 'mark', throw the dummy, walk back to the dog and then send the dog. I certainly used to do this myself until I realised that none of this is correct, because all this means it is not a 'mark'. A mark is a dummy or bird which has landed. The dog has seen or heard it and the handler sends the dog to retrieve almost immediately, from that place, *without anything else happening in between.* It is the last part of this sentence which is important. Nothing else should happen in between the dummy being thrown, landing, and the dog being sent, otherwise it is not a true 'mark' and one should not therefore send the dog on its name command.

If you leave your dog in a sit, walk forward, throw a dummy and then walk back to the dog something else *has* happened – you have walked back to the dog.

So, after the initial teaching of saying 'mark' and throwing a dummy from the dogs' side, yourself, do not do this again and always make sure someone else throws the dummy and says 'mark' once before throwing it. The dummy thrower can slap the dummy on their hand at the same time as saying 'mark' but should not say the word more that once.

The reason for this is that some dogs do not look up when 'mark' is shouted. Many dummy throwers then feel they should say 'mark' again, and this often gets to the ridiculous stage where a dummy thrower is saying 'mark' a dozen times, and the dog still does not look up. This is not what we want, after all a gun cannot shoot the same bird a dozen times, simply because 'my dog didn't see that'. So we need to teach the dog right from the start that they get one chance to see the dummy or bird and we are not going to hang around waiting until he decides he is ready to co-operate. Either he looks up, sees it and is sent, or he may have lost his chance. If the dog does not mark the dummy, the best thing to do is *send another dog*. Most dogs get this message much more readily!

So send another dog, or go and pick it up yourself, wait for a while and try again. Most dogs do not want one of their favourite activities taken away from them and they will usually do it perfectly the next time they are offered the opportunity. If not, the same procedure should be used and continue to be used, even if the dog does not get a single retrieve. You must not feel sorry for the dog. He will get a retrieve only if he plays the game your way, by your rules. It is your game, after all!

Make sure you have several dummies, some dogs have difficulties in always picking the same dummy and dummies also get wet from grass as well as the saliva from the dog and begin to be slimy and unpleasant. Have different types of dummy; small, large, sock dummies, dummy with pheasant wings attached, dummy with rabbit skin as well as tennis balls and make sure you also use other peoples dummies too. You do not want to teach a dog that he only picks dummies with your scent.

Having reached this stage it is important not to give too many retrieves to your dog and to maintain all your steadiness training you should always pick up more dummies and balls than you ever send the dog for. So one or two retrieves for the dog is ample and then you should throw other items which you and other people pick up, leaving your dog on a sit or just leave the items on the ground and do other exercises around them, with the dog ignoring the items.

Once the initial few marked retrieves have been achieved you should get a friend to throw dummies for you, if you are working on your own, or the alternative is only to do marks in a training group. Some dogs need to be taught that they still bring the dummy back to you even though someone else has thrown it and restricting marks to only when someone else throws the item for you, will also curb your own need, perhaps, to give the dog too many!

Being allowed to retrieve something should be seen by the dog as a treat, a reward at this stage and as with all treats, should be used sparingly otherwise it ceases to be a treat.

At this stage you need to be introducing the dog to the command 'hie lost'.

The definition of the 'hie lost' command to the dog is: Search and hunt the area approximately 6 feet in diameter from where you are.

This is the phrase which I use and you should find your own word or words and use it or them in this way forever. Some people use the word 'there' but I shall use the words 'hie lost throughout.

This is a command that cannot be taught other than by the dog learning for himself what it means. The primary use of the command is in a situation when you know where a dummy or bird is, but the dog does not.

To show the dog what the command means however it is necessary to use it to begin with, in conjunction with a dummy he can see and knows where it is. Once he gets used to the command, in that every time you say it he finds a dummy, he will begin to trust you and know that when you give the command he must hunt and then he will find the dummy. This element of trust is going to be crucial when you start sending your dog for blinds, which are dummies he has not seen thrown.

The 'hie lost' command should now be used every time you give your dog a marked retrieve but it should be used correctly, at the appropriate distance from the dummy, which is a radius of about 6 feet. You will remember, hopefully, that this is the personal space boundary for the dog!

Still keep the distances short for your dog. There is no point in a dummy being thrown a long distance if the dog does not have the confidence, skills and experience to do it properly. To build these things however, you should progress by keeping the distances roughly the same, but change the locations and terrain. This is then teaching the dog that the command means the same here, there and everywhere.

Practice should therefore include short marks on grass, in woodland, stubble, into cover (but not too dense, and not nettles or thick brambles at this stage) anywhere and everywhere you can find something different to increase the experience for your dog. You can also start to incorporate a mark over a small jump, through a hedge, over a ditch and anything suitable which is different so that the dog is also gaining experience of the 'get over' command coupled with a marked retrieve.

Increase all these experiences but do not increase the distances too much and you will have a dog which will be gaining many skills at working in as many different situations as possible and because the distances remain comfortable for the dog, he will grow in confidence, not only in himself, but in you, because this way he will not go wrong.

Part of this experience, as well as his continued learning that he cannot have every dummy he sees thrown but only the ones he is sent for, should include waiting whilst another dog retrieves a mark. This is more difficult if you are working on your own but in a class situation your dog will eventually be expected to sit off lead when a mark is thrown, but another dog will be sent. This experience needs to happen around this stage otherwise your dog may be thinking that it is either he or you who pick up all dummies. He needs to learn that yes it is sometimes him, sometimes it is you, but *sometimes it is one of several other dogs or one of several other people too.* He has to learn to be patient, he has to learn to watch and he has to learn that everything else he has been taught, applies in all circumstances so that *sit, means sit no matter what.* The new 'no matter what' must now include other dogs, other people and the fact that retrieving is allowed to be done by others.

Progress should now include further progress on walking in line with others combined with a mark when dogs and people will be retrieving whilst other dogs remain in a sit. Heelwork in line with others may now include a shot on occasions and should also include swift about turns to the right to mark dummies thrown behind the line.

🐾 (y) Water work

After a retrieve from water, the dog should get out of the water without shaking and return to the handler quickly, to present the dummy or bird.

(Photographs: Paul Lawrence)

CHAPTER EIGHTEEN

Developing work with water

Gundogs need to be able to swim on command and retrieve dead and wounded birds from in and across water as well as be able to hunt alongside water, in reeds, rushes, Water Lilies and other water cover areas. Swimming is one of the essential tasks of an adult, trained gundog whose role involves retrieving shot birds from difficult locations. Humans can pick up shot, dead birds from a grass field but recovering a wounded duck from reeds at the other side of a river, is not a task relished by most humans on a cold, winter day.

You are aiming with a water retrieve; to have a dog who will sit near water, off the lead. A dog who will mark down anything which lands on or the other side of water and who will, on command get straight into the water, swim, retrieve, get out of the water and return to you with the bird. You are also aiming to be able to command your dog to get into water, go in the direction you tell him, hunt a specific area, find and retrieve a bird *he may not have seen fall.*

To achieve this, all the components need to be perfected before the whole is assembled.

Retrieving which involves water, is really no different than a retrieve from any other area except for perhaps the challenges imposed by the water, such as fast current and hidden dangers below the surface. A handler, who has *not* taken control of a dog on land however, will have little chance of maintaining control of a dog when he is in, or on the other side, of water. Mainly because there is absolutely nothing a handler can do if a dog disobeys when there is a stretch of many yards of raging torrent between themselves and their dog! Unless of course, you are really into Olympic or Cross Channel swimming in a big way yourself!

We shall assume that you have a dog which is already confident playing in and around water. He may or may not be swimming, but your dog knows the 'heel', 'sit', 'hold' & 'give', 'leave it' and 'recall' commands. Your dog should have been taught the first stages of the 'get over' command, perhaps on low jumps or narrow ditches, as this command will start now, also to mean *negotiate the water obstacle in front of you.*

Attention, so far, to all the above means that your dog is steady and he should also be able to accomplish a simple 'mark' in a variety of different places and from various types of terrain, with a good return and present. If any of the above is not true, you should wait until any areas of difficulty have been attended to or you have given your dog more experience in these areas.

Training.

Take your dog to a suitable area of water and if possible, go with another handler and dog, or take someone with you willing to throw a dummy for you. It is sometimes useful to take an older, experienced dog but not essential and not advisable, unless this dog is totally reliable and steady. I like to take home-made water dummies for the first few sessions and use small diameter plastic bottles inserted in an old sock which you can knot at the top. Using these, means that any not retrieved, won't cost you a fortune to replace! You could also use the water toys used when first giving your dog water experience or any suitable objects which are safe, will float and will interest your dog. Having another dog present will be useful if you use dummies as the more experienced dog can then retrieve any of these for you, should the new recruit have difficulties.

When you begin, start with some heelwork, and a few exercises which you can do *near* the water. In this way you will use the water as a distraction in that the dog will be picking up the scent of the water, he will be perhaps hearing the different sounds made by it as well as possibly hearing and smelling the different wildlife present. All of these things will interest and possibly excite the dog and you need to be sure you remain in control and that your dog obeys the commands you give instantly, despite the new and interesting location. If there are any problems concerning disobedience to commands or if you have trouble in controlling the dog you should do some kind of exercises whereby you are in control, your dog obeys and then you should *go home.*

That means, having had a problem, do some basic exercises you know your dog understands, but you are in total control, have success on those exercises and then do no more! It is vital that the dog does not start to believe that he can please himself or does not have to obey you when his senses are telling him 'wow, this is very exciting and I'm off to investigate and have some fun'! Imagine adding to this; birds flying, gunshot, the scent of warm blood, birds being shot and dropping into the water!

If your dog is over stimulated at only the scent and sound of water now, he would be impossible to control given the additions! He will need careful, ongoing exposure to water, spread over a number of weeks perhaps, so it is important not to create problems now.

Most dogs simply accept that you are doing the things they already know but in a different place and the greater variety of different places you have managed to use for training, the better the dog seems to be. When you are certain you have control and your dog is obeying you instantly, on all your practice exercises, you can try a marked retrieve but with care – **do not go immediately and throw a dummy or anything into the water!**

Progress on land with marked retrieves should, by now, mean that you no longer throw dummies yourself for your dog to retrieve and you should therefore have someone else getting involved now.

To begin, position yourself a few yards away from the water. Have your dog sitting off lead in the heel position whilst the dummy thrower shouts 'mark' and throws a dummy on land, near the edge of the water. Your dog should remain steady. Praise him and remind him 'sit, good boy' and if all well, leave the dog and you go and pick up the dummy. Return to the dog and then have a dummy thrown just into the water so that it makes a splash and you go again to pick it up and return to the dog.

If all is well up to this point you will next be having a similar dummy thrown which you will send the dog for, but before this happens you need to think about your role.

Although the water at this stage may not appear to be much of an obstacle as such, this is the stage where you need to be putting in the command word of 'get over'. Hopefully you will have been using the 'hie lost' command too with your dog and the 'get over' command will have to be put in before the 'hie lost' for this exercise. This will be a marked retrieve where your dog will be sent on its name and the commands you will have to give are as follows: name, get over, hie lost, recall, hold, good boy, give, good boy, sit good boy.

Now because the distance is not very great you will have a lot of words to get out of your mouth in a very short space of time so to start it may be better to cut out the 'hie lost' command as it is the 'get over' command we need to introduce and is the most important. You may not have to give the 'hold' command when the dog returns to you but you need to be ready with the word on the edge of your tongue in case the dog looks as though he will drop the dummy.

If necessary, if you feel you will make a mess of it, revert to sending the dog on a 'hold' command. The commands would therefore be 'hold', 'get over', then recall if needed but remember to use 'hold' again when the dog is returning to you. You must remember not to grab the dummy, and should get down on the ground to praise the dog and scratch his chest before giving the dummy release command. You should then gain control by giving the dog a 'sit' command, and you walking round the dog back into the heel position. All this should be exactly the same as you have practiced before.

When you are ready, and have thought carefully about your job in this exercise, have a dummy thrown which is near the edge of the water and makes a splash then wait a second or two before sending the dog. If everything works well; that means you have given the correct commands, have acted appropriately, and the dog has done everything satisfactorily, then you could try one more mark of a similar kind, and then do no more with water for this session. Do a few more of your normal exercises near the water including throwing dummies which you pick up, and then finish.

Water work, as with all other work in training sessions, should not be the only thing practiced. All other exercises already learnt need to be incorporated into your training sessions and occasionally use some water training in amongst other training aspects.

Progress on subsequent sessions can then be made as follows:

- A dummy can be thrown slightly further into the water so that the dog will have to enter the water to retrieve it. This should not involve throwing the dummy into swimming depth water. The dog needs to build up confidence in entering shallow water and everything else, concerning the exercise, needs to be satisfactory in terms of steadiness, returning to you and presenting the dummy.
- At this stage another command can be included: that is the command of 'shake'. You may have already started including this word in previous months whenever your dog was wet and in the process of getting rid of water in his coat.

The 'shake' is another command, similar to 'hie lost' which cannot be taught so much as being learnt by the dog by association. When a dog is wet, and this does not always mean wet through, he wants to rid his coat of water as quickly as possible. The reason for this is that it feels uncomfortable but mainly because it slows him down. Carrying a gallon of water in the coat weighs quite a lot and his first instinct will tell him to shake it out.

Many dogs, if left to make this decision on their own, will shake several times in the process of working in water, they may loose birds by so doing, may drop birds and may come out of water and put a bird down, to shake. You need to take control of the shaking, right from the start and prevent the dog getting into a shaking habit which will be difficult to eradicate later. The dog's job is to bring dummies, and eventually birds, back to you quickly, and this means without shaking first. The dog needs to know however that he will be allowed to shake and it eventually becomes part of his reward for returning to you with the bird, releasing it on command, and then being able to shake. It is also an incentive to the dog to return to you as quickly as possible so that he can hand over the dummy and then shake.

If ever your dog is wet and is shaking water from his coat, say 'shake', or whatever word you choose; eventually your dog will shake on command, and this will be essential later.

- The next training session, return to the same area. Sit your dog in the same place as before, and have a dummy thrown in a similar place to last time, just into the water. Send the dog and complete the exercise but this time, after you have given the command for the dog to release the dummy, say 'shake' before you put the dog on a sit.

If you have a puppy which appears less than confident in, near and around water you will need to take care to build his confidence slowly. If you have an area of beach near water, you can try throwing a dummy sideways so the puppy has to run further but in the same depth of water, before trying to make him go deeper.

There is no point in being impatient with a puppy like this, all you can do is increase his exposure to water, let him gain experience with more play and do not associate it with having to do a retrieve other than perhaps once or twice. If you remain patient and keep the experience a positive one for the puppy, you will be doing all the right things, and with luck, one day the puppy will just dash into the water and show you that he is now ready to go further.

You will notice that none of the above has taken account of whether your dog had already managed to swim when he was being given early water experience.

Early water experience was to teach the dog about water.

Most of the exercises in this section have been to teach the dog that the commands you have taught him in other circumstances, apply too in connection with water. None of this so far, has needed to have the addition of swimming because until you are certain that the dog *is* obedient to all your commands and understands that this is simply a change of circumstances; there is no point in adding swimming to the situation.

When you get to the stage whereby your dog is working as well, in these circumstances, as he does on land when no water is involved, then it will be time to add a small amount of swimming. By this time, because every dog will be retrieving on command, with enthusiasm and accuracy, the question as to whether the dog was previously able to swim, is largely irrelevant.

Progress should then be made as follows:

- Have the dummy thrown into shallow water as before, but increase the distance you and the dog stand away from the water. This means the dog has to go a greater distance to retrieve the dummy, and a greater distance to return to you.
- Stand fairly close to the water and have the dummy thrown slightly further into the water. If your puppy can go into slightly deeper water, swim a few yards, retrieve, return to you,

present the dummy, shake and then sit, be impressed! Be pleased with yourself and your dog but do not get so carried away that you do too much.
- ☻ Next you should increase the distance you and the dog stand away from the water. The dog will have to go further to reach the water, the dummy will be thrown in the same place therefore the swimming distance will stay the same, giving the dog confidence, and he will then have further to run with the dummy, to return to you.
- ☻ Subsequent sessions can aim to build a little more swimming combined with extra distance on land.

Once your dog is swimming well and all other aspects are correct, do not do too many retrieves where the dummy is in the water. Aim for dummies over the other side of water.

If you do too many retrieves *in* water you may teach the dog that it is *only* in water that he must look. If you teach a dog always to cross water when you have said 'get over', when there is a dummy in the water, he will find it. The last thing you want, when a dummy is across the water on the other bank, is a dog swimming in ever decreasing or increasing circles round and round a lake. He needs to get in, get across the water quickly, and hunt the opposite bank.

Further work with water will need to be accomplished once the dog has learned other things, particularly directional work on land. You can then begin to incorporate water with all directional commands.

Problems

For those who may have puppies or older dogs which appear to be reluctant swimmers, there are things you can try to help them:

- ☻ Take the puppy with an older dog, or with other puppies, and let them play together in water - it sometimes works and sometimes does not.

🐾 Paddle yourself in deeper water, or go swimming – it sometimes works, and sometimes does not.

Anything may work but I think it is largely a question of exposing the puppy to water as much as possible and then, hopefully their retrieving urge will take over and it is this which may take them into the water and swimming, more than anything. Many dogs, like humans, will not go into water just to swim. I believe some dogs just do not see any point in it. Other dogs prefer going into water, just for the sheer pleasure of it all and will swim for a long time with nothing to retrieve.

Some cautious puppies do better on streams where they can learn to cross water or larger expanses of very shallow water where they can run for a long way through it. Just try every opportunity which comes your way, but without putting pressure on the puppy.

Problems with water retrieves usually occur concerning a dog perhaps dropping a dummy, or in shaking. For dropping, further work may need to be done concerning the 'hold' command and teaching the dog that 'hold' means hold no matter what the circumstances. Sometimes this can be improved at home by going back to your receptacle for water. Put a dummy into water and get the dog to retrieve from the water without going into it. Then do more work near and just into water and never move on a stage until everything is right.

If you are having problems regarding the dog shaking before the dummy has been presented to you, this occurs frequently when the dog first gets out of the water, after picking the dummy. In this case, set up a retrieve in the water and then you go to the water's edge and meet the dog coming out. Frequently putting in a 'No' just when you believe the dog is *thinking* of shaking, will be enough to stop the dog doing it. Also, putting your hand on top of the dog's head as he is coming out of the water may stop him shaking, but you may have to do some or all of these things each time for a while until the dog understands he must not shake until he has presented the dummy to you.

The important thing is to try and nip any problems in the bud. Do not let the dog display any problem more than once. The once should be enough for you to work out how to prevent, what may be a slight mistake, from increasing to a major problem.

Do not fall into the trap of believing that any problem you see will disappear on its own, so try not to ignore anything which may not be quite right. If you do nothing about it, the dog will assume he is to continue with whatever action he is taking. Non-intervention by a human is taken as permission to carry on doing something, by a dog. Before you know it, once that permission, as seen by the dog, is worked on by the dog, the slightly not quite right aspect will have been developed by him into a major work of art and it will not be to your taste!

CHAPTER NINETEEN

The 'go back' command

The 'go back' command is the first of what we call directional commands. These are the commands which enable us to send the dog, where we want the dog to go. They are not to do with retrieving as such but to do with the journey, or how the dog will get to where the retrieve is.

The Definition of this command to the dog is: Go away from me (the handler) in a straight line.

Some people use the command of 'get out' for this and it does not matter which command you choose to attach to the meaning, provided you decide and then continue with this for life. I shall use the words 'go back' throughout.

To begin the 'go back' training the dog needs to be able to: walk to heel off the lead, sit steadily whilst you walk away and whilst other things may be happening, hold and present a dummy correctly on a marked retrieve and understand a recall. If none or only some of the above aspects are true, then you should leave this training exercise until later whilst you correct any problems in other areas.

Training.

You will need to find a training area with a track or pathway so that you can teach your dog to work in a straight line. If you cannot find something suitable an alternative would be to find a hedge-line, fence or wall to work against so that at least one side will be a guide. You will also need to have 2 or 3 puppy dummies and your whistle.

To begin:

- 🐾 Have a dummy in your hand and your whistle in your mouth, with the dog off lead in the heel position on a sit.
- 🐾 Then, give your dog a 'heel' command, walk a few paces, stop, and give your dog a 'sit' command, either by whistle or verbally.
- 🐾 Shout 'mark', tap the dummy on your hand and throw the dummy a few feet away, in a straight line in front of you. Your dog should remain steady. Let your dog mark the fall of the dummy and then say 'heel'; do an about turn with the dog, walk one or two paces and then stop, giving your dog a 'sit' command
- 🐾 Leave your dog on a sit, walk 2 paces away and then turn to face your dog.
- 🐾 At this point wait a few seconds. Look behind the dog to see where the dummy is in relation to the dog. When looking beyond the dog to where the dummy is lying; if the dummy is to the right of the dog, from your view-point, you will need to use your right hand; if the dummy is to the left of the dog, from your view point, you will need to use your left hand. The dog will be facing you and will have to turn round before going back. The dummy will therefore be slightly left, if you have used your left hand, or slightly right if you have used your right hand to the dog when he has turned. (This all sounds more complicated when written down, but one of those situations which are *easier done than said!*)
- 🐾 Hopefully, the dummy is directly behind your dog, in which case it does not matter which hand you use. When you have decided which hand is appropriate, blow your stop whistle (to mean 'look at me, I'm going to tell you what to do) and at the same time put the appropriate hand and arm up as high as you can. Drop your arm and then immediately raise it back to the same position and say 'Go Back'.

- The dog should turn on the spot and go to the dummy. When the dog is approaching the dummy, say 'hie lost'. The dog should then pick up the dummy and return to you with a correct present.

Problems.

There are several areas where you may have problems:

- If there are any problems concerning heelwork, sit or steadiness you should leave this exercise for a while and correct any areas as appropriate.
- If the problem concerns your dummy throwing, take some dummies out and practice throwing them accurately. Do this on your own without the dog. If you still cannot throw the dummy in a straight line a few feet, then it would be best just to leave the dog and go out in front, tap the dummy on your hand, say 'mark', and place the dummy on the ground.
- If the dog runs in when you throw the dummy, go back to the exercise where you sit the dog up and throw dummies around him, picking them up yourself. Then try some heel work off lead, and throw dummies when you and the dog are walking. You should make sure your dog is steady and understands he must not do anything other than sit, if that is the command he has been given.
- Occasionally dogs will not understand the 'go back' command when you first use it. This is understandable because they have never heard it before. There is no point in getting cross with the dog but do try and make it easier for the dog to understand. Stand closer to the dog when facing him and encourage him back. If necessary, run back with him, praising him and then try the exercise again. You can also try leaving the dog much closer to the dummy, so throw the dummy, turn on the spot, and then just stand in front of the dog. Do not give the command more than once because as with all

other commands you need to teach the dog that he must obey the first and only command he is given.

- A difficulty some handlers have is that they are reluctant to hold their hand and arm straight up above their heads. Some handlers put their hand in front of their shoulder, by bending the arm at the elbow and then try moving the hand and arm, still bent, forward from the body – almost in a pushing motion, with the verbal 'go back' command. This, whilst being perfectly adequate as a hand signal whilst a dog is sitting a yard in front, is woefully inadequate when the dog is sitting the other side of a field. The reason it is inadequate, is that the hand signal cannot be seen by the dog. In bright sunlight, or at dusk with the handler dressed in dark green, which blends into the surrounding trees, as well as looking very similar to another, the dog cannot see what you are trying to communicate. He may not be able to hear you, but he should be able to see what you want him to do. Changing your body shape is the only way your dog can do this. I have even seen handlers trying this with hands wrapped in green gloves against a background of a green coat and whilst it may be good for the handler to be correctly attired and colour co-ordinated, it does nothing to help their unfortunate dog waiting to be given some kind of help as to what is required of him. So, for your hand signal to have some impact, your body shape needs to change.

- Try the exercise 2 or 3 times on the first occasion and then leave the dog to think about it for a few days before trying again. Just go on teaching the dog with patience what you require, and one day, the dog will simply turn round, get the dummy and all will be well.

- Some dogs take quite a while to understand that they should turn immediately when given the 'go back' command and many puppies come forward to their handler before turning and going back for the dummy. You just need to be patient. Sometimes with this problem, getting someone else to throw the dummy may solve the problem.

Once your dog is doing this exercise perfectly you should start increasing the distances.

At the start, it is easier to keep the distance between the dog and the dummy, fairly short. The dog knows where the dummy is, and this will give him confidence, so increase the distance first by leaving the dog in the same position but you walk further away from the dog before sending him. Once your dog is confident with this, you can start increasing the distance by moving with the dog further away from the dummy after you have turned. In this way the dog has to turn and go back further.

Have another person throw the dummy on occasions as this can increase the distance the dummy is thrown initially, as well as being useful experience for the puppy in understanding he must bring the dummy back to the handler. Many puppies think they should take it to the person who has thrown it!

After a few sessions you may find the dog is beginning to anticipate what you are going to tell him, he may start turning round before you give the command, saying 'I know, what to do'. That will be your sign to change the exercise, and show the dog that 'you may know what to do, but it's going to be different this time'. You also need to change the exercise and develop it further with a dog who does not begin to anticipate, but has learnt how to do it perfectly so far.

Start the exercise as usual but when you turn to face the dog, give him the 'sit and watch me' whistle and hand signal but then, instead of the 'go back' command, recall him instead.

When you first try this, it is better to have someone else throwing the dummy for you. In this way, if the dog should disobey your recall whistle, the dummy thrower should immediately pick up the dummy and therefore prevent the dog from retrieving it. The dog disobeyed, and should not therefore be allowed to have the dummy. As most dogs are quicker than their handlers, most handlers would not be able to get to the dummy before the dog! Unless of course, you are a Gold Medal Olympic standard sprinter!

The dummy thrower should be ready to pick up the dummy if necessary, but you need to feel confident that the dog will obey you when you recall him. If you expect him to disobey, he will probably oblige! Expect him to obey, and he probably will!

Blow your whistle command of 'sit and watch me' followed by your recall whistle and when the dog returns to you praise him, put him on a sit and then you walk round into the heel position. Give him a heel command and then do an about turn on the spot and put the dog on a sit in the heel position facing the dummy.

If all is well, you are now going to show the dog another way of doing a 'go back'. The meaning is the same 'go away from me in a straight line' but this time the dog will be going from the heel position instead of from out in front of you.

Bend down so you are on a level with the dog and put your right arm and hand down so that your arm is parallel with his face, with your hand out-stretched, straight and pointing directly at the dummy. In this way the dog should be looking along your arm to your hand in the direction of the dummy. When he is looking on the correct line, leave your hand in position and say 'go back'.

Most dogs at this stage will do exactly that.

Be careful not to move your arm and hand and do not stand up straight until your dog has moved away from you. Many handlers throw their arm to the side when giving the verbal command and their dog goes out to the right instead of in a straight line.

Practice the 'go back' from both positions and keep the dog guessing so he does not anticipate, but waits for you to command him.

Problems.

- 🐾 Some dogs, when given the recall command, instead of the 'go back' command they were expecting, may stay rooted to the spot – another 'good fault', in that it means the dog is a bit confused, and rather than do the wrong thing, he waits where he is. Encourage rather than punish although you should give a growl and then repeat the recall command, and crouch down if necessary. Make sure you praise excessively when the dog *starts* to get up. This will reassure him.
- 🐾 On the 'go back' from the heel position, if your dog is reluctant to leave you because he does not understand, go with him, run and make it exciting and then try again by shortening the distance until he understands.
- 🐾 If your dog disobeys the recall whistle, turns to go back, and the dummy is picked up by the dummy thrower, you will need to set up the exercise again in exactly the same way. If necessary do it up to 3 times and then do no more. Let the dog think about it for a day or two and then try again. You will then find your dog will probably do it correctly. If not, try another 3 times, and keep following the same pattern of 3 times, do no more, leave it for a few days and then try again, but do not move on until you can go out, set up the exercise, and your dog does it correctly. You should then proceed with the 2nd half of the exercise and continue as below.
- 🐾 Regardless of the fact that this exercise concerns the 'go back' command, if the recall is a problem, this should be practiced separately and perfected before the 'go back' training is taken further. Frequently the problem is with the handler so make sure you are giving precise and clear commands consistently.
- 🐾 Some people also have problems when they try to do the recall part of this exercise, because they have given the 'go

back' command in the first part of the exercise, before the dog is looking at them. Remember that the stop whistle before giving the 'go back' command is to mean 'continue sitting, watch me, because I am going to tell you what to do.' You must therefore wait until the dog looks at you before giving the command – however long that takes! If you do have a dog reluctant to look at you, make sure you give him verbal praise when he does look at you. Also make sure you are smiling! Some handlers, if they have to wait for a dog to look at them, then have a scowl upon their face – no wonder the dog doesn't want to look at them!

Once the dog is doing both parts of the exercise correctly you can start increasing the distances and then after a few more sessions you should be able to walk across a field, throw a dummy, walk back across the field with the dog and then send him back for the dummy.

Mix up the order in which you do the exercise so that sometimes you leave the dog at a distance and send him straight back, and sometimes recall him. Keep the dog guessing, make sure he does not anticipate what you want, and that he waits until you give him a command. Also make sure you do not always do long distances when practicing. Sometimes you should do a short 'go back' too.

Most dogs love doing 'go backs' but you need to remember that you are teaching the dog to go away from you in a straight line so you need to line yourself up with the dummy before sending the dog. Practice on a track or along a hedge line and don't be tempted to send a dog diagonally across an open field. Keep it simple.

Increase the distances then give the dog experience of the same command in different circumstances such as in a wood, stubble fields, anywhere which will give the dog more experience and therefore increase his confidence. You can then try putting the dummy into a bit of cover so he will have to hunt for it when he has gone back or combine a 'go back' with some water work.

Remember that at this stage your dog should always see where the dummy is thrown, and know where it is, even if he has to hunt a small area when he gets there. You want the dog to understand what 'go back' means, in all circumstances, and for him to learn that the command always means the same, even if the surroundings and the terrain changes.

Part of this increased experience should also involve waiting. Do not be in too much of a hurry to send the dog. He needs to sit patiently until you decide to give him the command and it is also important to build up the dog's memory so that he can remember for longer, where a dummy is and what he is supposed to be doing.

If you are able to work alongside other handlers and dogs, build the exercise up so that perhaps 2, 3 or more dummies are put out and send each of two, three, or more dogs, one at a time with the other dogs waiting patiently and obediently for their turn. Make sure you vary whose turn it is!

The 'go back' command is arguably the most important directional command you can teach and it is obedience to this command which you will find the most useful.

The goal you are aiming for, with this command, is to be able to point the dog in the correct direction from the heel position, give the 'go back' command and the dog to go, at speed in a straight line *forever* - well, until you command him to do something else!

In many situations this will bring the dog to the bird or dummy with no further commands being necessary. For more complicated journeys you may have to stop the dog at some point and direct either to the left or right but if your dog will at least go the required distance initially, the majority of ultimate retrieves will be relatively simple.

CHAPTER TWENTY

The 'Get on' command.

A great deal of the work for a gundog will be retrieving dead and wounded birds from a starting position by the handler's side other than when they are perhaps hunting on a freer basis when sweeping up after a drive. This means, in practice, that the handler may be standing behind or along side the guns with their dog in the heel position, off lead, in a sit, waiting and watching a drive.

Shoots can differ in respect of whether: the dogs are picking all the shot birds during the drive, or just picking wounded birds or not picking any birds until a drive is over. On most shoots the practice is that the wounded birds are picked as soon as possible so that the bird can be dispatched quickly to prevent further suffering. This means that a dog will be sent: from the handler's side on a 'name' command, such as when the dog has seen the bird land, and the dog is sent immediately with nothing else happening in between, which is a marked retrieve; or the handler lines the dog up in the direction of where the bird landed and the dog is sent on a 'go back' command.

Having begun training on the 'go back' command, you and the dog will be beginning to understand that the 'go back' is a command which can be used either from the heel position, or when the dog is at a distance from the handler and therefore has to turn round and go away from the handler in a straight line.

The 'get on' command is another directional command, but is a command which is only ever used when the dog is at a distance from the handler. It can never be used when the dog is in the heel position.

To begin training for this command your dog needs to be steady, and needs to be at the stage of understanding the 'go back' command from both positions i.e. at a distance from the handler (facing the handler), and from the heel position (facing in the same direction as the handler). The dog should be able to go a considerable distance to retrieve the dummy from both positions and be able to remember where the dummy is.

The definition of the 'Get on' command to the dog is: Go in a straight line either right or left, depending on which arm I use.

This is the phrase I use. You must decide which command you are going to use and then keep to this for life. Some people use the command 'get out' but this can only be used if it has not been used instead of a 'go back' command and it does not really matter which words you decide to use but the command should make a different sound from any other command. I shall use the words 'get on' throughout.

Training.

The training for this command is best set up in a similar way to that used when teaching the 'go back' command, when a fence or track was used to ensure the dog learned about going in a straight line. The only difference, being that you should find a fence or hedge line whereby the dog has a straight line *behind* him because he now needs to learn about taking a straight line to the side, either to the right or to the left. So find a suitable area where you can sit the dog in front of a straight line. Whether it is a hedge, fence, or wall does not matter and if you cannot find anything like this a straight piece of track or path will suffice and you can use the back edge of the pathway as your straight line. You will need 2 dummies for this exercise.

Start by positioning the dog in a sit with his back to the straight edge. Remind the dog 'sit, good boy' and take two or three paces past your dog and turn to face him. This is not new to the dog, as this has been the start of numerous parts of training and he should remain steady.

Fence/wall.
_____

                              D (dog)

                              H (handler)

Remind your dog to sit, either verbally with a hand signal, or with a whistle command and hand signal, and then throw a dummy to your right, saying 'mark' as you throw it. You need to make sure that you throw the dummy with accuracy so that the dummy lands in a straight line with the dog, a few yards away to the right as you are looking at it. If you are not proficient at dummy throwing by this stage, then it would be wise to get someone else to throw it for you!

Then proceed as follows.

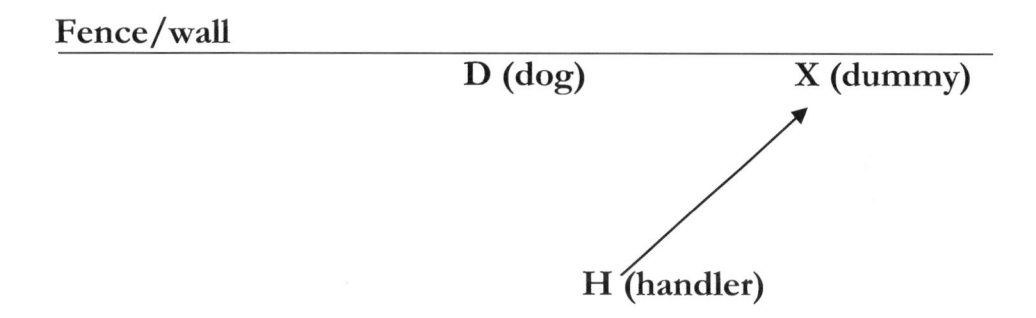

Fence/wall
_____

                  D (dog)   **X (dummy)**

                         H (handler)

- 🐾 Your dog should remain in position whilst you throw the dummy and he should watch to see where it lands. Wait a few seconds, and then hold your right hand and arm up above your head and blow your stop whistle (to mean remain in a sit and look at me I'm going to tell you what to do).
- 🐾 Your dog should look at you when you blow your whistle and when he does, say 'good boy', praising him for looking at you and waiting to be told what is going to happen.

- You should then drop your arm, bend it at the elbow, and immediately move it out to the right in a straight line at 90 degrees from your body. At the same time, say 'get on'.
- Hopefully, your dog will move to his left and pick up the dummy. When the dog starts to move towards the dummy, you should give the 'hie lost' command as he is approaching the dummy, or give a 'hold' command and this will reassure him he is doing the right thing. When he has the dummy in his mouth, use your recall whistle to get the dog to come straight back to you, or use a verbal command of 'come'.
- When the dog returns to you praise him but do not take the dummy too quickly. Praise first, then take control by giving the dog a sit command, take the dummy with the appropriate release command and make sure you maintain control of the situation by reminding the dog to sit. You should then walk to the right of the dog and back into the heel position.

If all went well, give your dog a heel command and walk back with the dog and position him again in the same place, leaving him as before. Follow the same procedure as at the start but this time throw the dummy to the left and send the dog with your left arm signal and the 'get on' verbal command.

If your dog does a right and then a left 'get on' do not do any more on that training session, do some other exercises and then finish and let the dog think about it for a day or two.

There are a few problems handlers may have with this exercise:

- If your dog is unsteady, that is if he moves from the sit position at any stage, either when you first leave him or when you throw the dummy, then these issues should be addressed separately. Do not try this exercise again until you have done some more work as appropriate.

- 🐾 If the dog does not move out to the side instantly, and he may not as this is a new command, pick up the dummy yourself and start again but, this time, stand closer to the dog so that you are just in front, facing him. Follow the same procedure. Encourage the dog to go to his left and if necessary, take sideways steps to the right yourself until you are level with the dummy and then say 'hie lost' or 'hold'. Practice this same exercise without any changes until your dog will go in the correct direction on command, and then try throwing a dummy to the left instead until the dog will go one side or another, on command, with you a few paces away.
- 🐾 If your dog comes towards you, you are standing too far away. Pick up the dummy yourself and start again, standing immediately in front of your dog. Do not move further away until your dog is moving correctly to the side, and then increase the distance gradually.
- 🐾 If the problem is in your dummy throwing, go out and practice, without the dog, until you can get it in the correct place. If you are unable to perfect this, get a friend to throw the dummy for you, or go out and place the dummy each time.

Your first few training sessions should concentrate on throwing only one dummy at a time, either to the left or to the right, and practice until the dog is moving instantly on command in both directions. Then try increasing the distance, first between yourself and the dog and then, when all is going well, increase the distance between the dog and the dummy.

It will then be time to take things a little further.

Sit the dog as usual and take up a position in front of the dog, a few paces away. Throw one dummy to the right and another dummy to the left. This is a new situation for the dog, as he has never seen two dummies being thrown in this exercise before and you will find that the dog will probably concentrate on the last dummy thrown. He will almost certainly continue to look at the dummy on *his* right, but you are going to send him for the one to *his* left, which was the first dummy to be thrown. You should blow your stop whistle (a reminder to continue sitting and to watch you), and use your right arm to give the hand signal. You should not do anything else at this stage until your dog looks at you. Once your dog looks at you, drop your arm and give him the right 'get on' command.

Hopefully, your dog will go immediately to his left and retrieve the dummy, as this is what he already knows.

When you first try with two dummies thrown, some dogs will think they have to fetch both. Because you have practiced, the dog will probably go, without hesitation, for the dummy you want. It is only when he has the first dummy in his mouth that he suddenly thinks to himself, 'hang on a minute my lad, there is another dummy out here somewhere.' His reaction to this thought may well be to go and look for or try to retrieve the other dummy too. This is not what we want. His job, as soon as he has something in his mouth, is to return to you quickly.

To avoid any such problem, once the dog is going out to his left for the first dummy thrown, move towards where the dog *was*. That means you go forward and take up a central position where the dog was sitting originally. You should then turn to face the returning dog. This will mean that after picking the dummy, the dog comes back to you in the centre instead of on the diagonal line.

This position puts you on a direct line to the other dummy. You will therefore be able to stop him from heading off to the second dummy, if necessary, and it will help you keep control of the situation. Not all dogs will try to go to the other dummy, but prevention is easier than correction after the event.

When the dog has successfully retrieved the dummy, position him again, and then you go and pick up the remaining dummy.

Start again and this time, throw one dummy to the left and one dummy to the right. This time you will find the dog will probably concentrate on the dummy on his *left,* but you are going to send him for the one on his *right,* the first dummy thrown. Follow the same procedure, but use your left arm for both the initial 'stop/look at me' whistle and for the subsequent 'get on' command.

On subsequent training sessions you can stop moving into the centre, provided everything is going well. Once the dog is going confidently for the correct dummy, every time, with no steadiness problems or going in the wrong direction, it will be time to change the exercise slightly.

Once a dog understands this exercise, there is a danger that he starts to assume that when you put two dummies out, the next thing to happen is that he is sent to retrieve. That has been true as a means of enabling the dog to understand what the 'get on' command means. He needs to understand at this stage however, that even though he is at a distance from you, and even though there is a dummy thrown out, or 2 dummies out, it does not always follow that he will be given the 'get on' command.

Throw one dummy to either the left or the right, blow your stop whistle, and then blow a recall whistle instead. Make sure you are in a position, should it be necessary, to get to the dummy before the dog. He must not have the dummy if you have recalled him. It is often useful to have a friend standing by who can pick up the dummy for you should the dog fail to recall, but they need to be quick and make sure they get to the dummy before the dog!

There is no need to put a recall in very often but it is important to reinforce the obedience rules before you establish in the dog's mind that there is only one way of doing this exercise.

Progress can then be made as follows:

- 🐾 Once your dog is able to retrieve a left or a right dummy on command but with two dummies out, vary the exercise by throwing 2 dummies and then put in a recall command.
- 🐾 Practice sending the dog for a left or a right dummy no matter in which order you have thrown them. It is important to do this, now and again, to make sure you are not teaching the dog that he should always go for the first dummy thrown. He needs to learn that he should always go for the dummy *you* want.
- 🐾 When your dog is doing all this well, then aim to send the dog for two dummies. In case anyone has any doubts about this, I hasten to add that this means *one at a time!* After the dog has retrieved the 1st dummy, you will need to re-position him on the centre spot again before sending him for the 2nd dummy. Do this first and then try re-throwing the 1st dummy before the dog retrieves the 2nd.

Build up gradually and never do more than one or two at each session. You should try to increase the distances gradually too; firstly by increasing the distance between yourself and the dog, thus showing the dog that you are still in control whatever the distance between you; and then increase the distances between the dog and the dummies. You can throw one dummy very close to the dog and one dummy at a greater distance, sending him first for the one furthest away. Try as many variations as you can and practice the exercise in as many different locations as you can find.

When furthering experience on marked retrieves and water work, you can also try leaving your dog at a suitable distance and incorporating a 'get on', in one direction or another into water or onto different terrain. All this will increase the experience for the dog as well as increase his understanding that circumstances will change, but the meaning of commands will never change and must be obeyed *no matter what!*

CHAPTER TWENTY-ONE

Blinds.

A 'blind' is the word used to describe a dummy, bird or any item which the dog is required to retrieve, but which the dog has either not seen or sometimes, not heard it thrown, fall or shot. Because the dog has not seen the item, this type of retrieve is sometimes called an 'unseen' by some people, rather than a 'blind'.

Any retrieve, whereby the dog has not been alerted to the fact that something has landed on the ground, is therefore called a blind/unseen retrieve. There are however, other retrieves which need to be treated by the handler as though they were blinds to the dog. This aspect is often confusing for novice handlers and I will therefore explain.

You will remember that one of the factors which constitutes a 'marked' retrieve, when the dog is sent to retrieve on its name, is that *nothing else happens in between.* This means that for a mark, you and the dog see and/or hear the mark and you send the dog for it, from that spot, almost immediately and nothing has happened between the item landing and you sending the dog.

Imagine that you and the dog see one bird shot and fall to the ground, and before you can send the dog, another bird is shot and falls to the ground. You and the dog would probably turn to see the second bird fall. You then need to consider the situation; supposing you realise that the second bird shot is dead but the first bird shot is still alive?

You now have, effectively, two marks but neither should be *treated* as marks in terms of how you should command your dog to retrieve them.

You need to send the dog to retrieve the first bird shot, as this one is still alive and must be dispatched quickly, but you cannot treat it as a 'mark' because something *has* happened in between. In fact, several things have happened in between: another shot or several shots have been fired, another bird has been shot, you have moved to observe the fall of the second bird shot and there has been a time lapse whilst this was happening and you were deciding what to do.

If you treat this whole situation as a mark and simply say the dog's name, the dog will almost certainly go and retrieve the second bird shot as this is the one which will be on his mind. You don't want that bird to be retrieved first; you need the first bird which was shot. Both birds should therefore be treated as though they were blinds. All this is for later however.

As far as training is concerned, this is the first time you can seriously consider the *journey* part of a retrieve. At this point, a dog will be going from you on command, and he has no idea what he is going for, where he is going to, or why he is being sent.

Training, concerning any types of retrieve when teaching your dog directional commands, has necessitated dummies being thrown as marks and initially being totally visible to the dog. This has been true whether you have been throwing dummies you pick up, others pick up, for marked retrieves, marked retrieves for other dogs, teaching the 'go back' command, teaching the 'get on' command and perhaps when water was involved.

The use of dummies and other items has been used as a catalyst for helping the dog understand the meaning of certain commands associated with retrieving. We have used these items to let the dog see something exciting: (a) as part of steadiness training when teaching the dog he was not allowed to have things he wanted, unless given permission; and (b) to teach specific commands such as his name used for a mark, as well as the 'go back' and 'get on' commands.

Up to this point therefore the dog has only left you on command from your side or moved on command when at a distance from you, *after* he has actually seen something thrown or placed. This acted as an encouragement or incentive for him to go where you wanted him to go, thus helping him to learn the particular command involved.

Previous training in this way was nothing to do with the dummy. The dummy, in itself was unimportant as it was the directional teaching which was the key element. Whether the dog retrieved the dummy was largely irrelevant as long as the dog went in the direction commanded.

Before you try to do any work on blinds it is important that your dog is managing to do simple marked retrieves properly, which means he is steady whilst a dummy is thrown, waits until you given the name command to leave you, will go straight to the fall, find the dummy, come straight back to you and present the dummy properly.

It is also important that the dog understands and obeys a 'go back' command from at a distance and facing you, and from your side in the heel position.

Your dog should be enthusiastic when working with you and you should have built up a good bond of trust with your dog so that he is obeying your commands instantly and willingly and there are no outstanding areas of difficulty on aspects of training tackled so far.

If none or only some of this is true, you should work on any areas of difficulty first before trying this new piece of training. All dogs differ in their rate of learning and it is much better to continue doing things the dog already knows, and build on confidence and experience already achieved, rather than push a dog before he is ready.

To do even a simple blind retrieve the dog is going into the unknown, for he knows not what and he has to leave the one person in whom so far, he has put his trust, without knowing why.

This is quite a mile-stone for a puppy or young dog!

Training.

To begin training it is preferable to have someone with you who can place dummies for you. It is possible to put out blind retrieves yourself if you train on your own but not as easy or effective unless you put the dog out of sight each occasion and you can only do this later on, not at the beginning.

Work concerning blinds is different from the way marked retrieves are done in that you can do marks by throwing the dummy yourself, only in the very beginning, and never after this. With blinds it is better to have someone else put the dummy out in the beginning, and then you can do it yourself, with certain precautions and provisos, in the later stages.

Working on blinds does not involve any new commands. This is simply a 'go back' with a difference!

So far your dog will have learnt and understood that the 'go back' command means to go away from you in a straight line. You will have already begun to help the dog in terms of the angle of this straight line when the dog is at a distance from you, by using the left or right hand and arm signal, to mean go back slightly left or slightly right.

When sending the dog from your side, you will have been lining the dog up with your hand and arm pointing at the dummy. Your dog will have therefore been picking up, albeit subtle, clues concerning the location of a dummy, which he has seen, but above all he will be learning that you are to be trusted because he has always found something when he goes in the direction commanded.

Blind retrieves depend on the trust that the dog has in his handler and leader, because the dog is setting off on a journey and he has no clue why he is going and has no clue about the purpose or ending. It is important for this first journey into the unknown to be of short duration with a successful and happy ending! Remember that this is the first time your dog has had to leave you and go anywhere on command, without the incentive of seeing a dummy, so keep it simple, and have success.

Set up a short, and simple, marked retrieve onto short grass or area where the dummy will not be hidden and send the dog in the usual way on his name command. When the dog has retrieved this mark and is on the way back to you, the dummy thrower should place another dummy in exactly the same place, without the dog seeing or hearing this being done.

When the marked dummy has been retrieved and presented properly, get your dog back into the heel position, on a sit facing the same way as before, and then line yourself and the dog up to face where the 'blind' dummy has been placed. You should adopt the same position as with a 'go back' from your side with your hand and arm pointing on a line with the dummy.

Keeping your hand and arm still, and with the dog looking down the correct line, say 'go back'. Your dog should leave your side immediately and, going on the correct line, should arrive at the correct location, at which point you should say 'hie lost' until your dog finds the dummy. If necessary put in a 'hold' command, followed by a recall and the usual present.

Most handlers and dogs have no problems with this provided that sufficient work and progress has been made on developing the 'go back' command. Some dogs are a little hesitant to leave their handler initially, as they do not understand the new situation. You will need to encourage such dogs and if necessary run with them all the way to the dummy and then give a 'hie lost' command. It is important however, not to repeat the 'go back' command because as with all other commands you want the dog to obey the first and only command given. Encourage as much as you can, let the dog find the dummy and then set up the exercise again in exactly the same way, in exactly the same place.

I think I have only ever had to do this twice with any puppy and by the time you do it a third time, the puppy will be leaving your side immediately on its own.

If you have a dog which is a little reluctant to leave you, and you have had to go with the dog as above, it is important to remember that this exercise is to focus on *the journey* and not the retrieve.

Some handlers loose the plot on occasions and, having run out with the dog, they pick up the dummy, say 'mark' and then throw the dummy for the dog to retrieve. I believe you should not do this because you will be teaching the dog nothing appropriate.

All that would do is to teach the dog 'when I say 'go back', and you haven't seen a dummy thrown, I will run out with you. I shall pick up the dummy, say 'Mark' and you can retrieve the dummy and you will have seen it thrown'.

The dog will have learnt nothing about the journey, or about 'blinds' and you may well cause problems on work and standards already achieved on 'marks'. So take your time, don't change the exercise and give the dog the chance to learn what you are teaching.

It takes as long as it takes for the dog to learn!

Whether your dog does it correctly on the 1st, 2nd or 3rd time, do not do it again after the first correct one or after the third one where you have to encourage all the way. Let the dog think about the new aspect of the 'go back' for a few days then try again, in exactly the same way.

I realise I am repeating myself frequently in urging you, whenever there is a problem on any exercise, to do it again in *exactly the same way!* I say this because so often I see handlers who, when trying to teach their dog and the dog does not grasp the lesson immediately, change the exercise. I have no problem in splitting the exercise into smaller pieces when necessary, but the goal of the exercise should always remain as the focus.

Imagine that somebody is trying to tell you something complicated and you have only heard part of what they are saying. Whilst you are trying to make sense of what you *have* heard, you ask the person to repeat what they said. If the person repeats the entire statement exactly as before, you will be able to fill in the bits you did not hear, and make sense of the whole. If, however, the person then says something entirely different the whole process will be impossible for you; you will be unable to fill in the missing gaps from the first statement, and will consequently not really hear the second statement either. The first person will then either have to tell you again, or go away muttering about how stupid you are!

If a handler does the equivalent when trying to teach a dog something i.e. tries once, the dog does not grasp it, so the handler changes the exercise; the dog must get totally frustrated.

The handler does not know which bits the dog has grasped and by not doing the exercise in exactly the same way, the dog is unable to fill in the gaps for himself. Dogs being dogs, the sensible ones probably then give up trying to understand whereas if the dog had been shown the same thing just one more time, he probably would have got it sorted!

Handlers need to be patient and be prepared to do it again and again, exactly the same, until the dog understands what you want.

Once your dog has achieved this first stage of leaving you, finding the dummy and returning with it to you, you will be able to go further with the exercise. Future developments should continue with a blind placed in the same place as a previous mark but you should aim to increase the distances and then start to throw and place dummies into cover, so the dog has to hunt; or throw and place dummies round a corner, behind a bush, anywhere suitable which is going to increase the experience and confidence of the dog. This will all tell you that the dog is not only obeying you but has the confidence to leave your side and go further away from you as well as being able to work out of sight too.

You can also check whether your dog understands the full meaning of the 'hie lost' command by putting the second, blind dummy within a 6 foot diameter of the first marked dummy so that the dog has to hunt a wider area in *almost* the same place.

When your dog has the confidence to work in this way, it will be time to take things a little further and that will be to have blinds placed when there has been no previous mark thrown.

It is important at this stage not to try and start at the sort of distances you had built up on the marks and blinds because you want the dog to understand the further meaning of the 'go back' in as simple a way possible and without the dog going wrong. It is advisable therefore to aim to find a track or pathway when you first try this exercise.

Plan before hand, and aim if possible for the placing of the dummy to be made in the opposite direction from which the dummy will be retrieved.

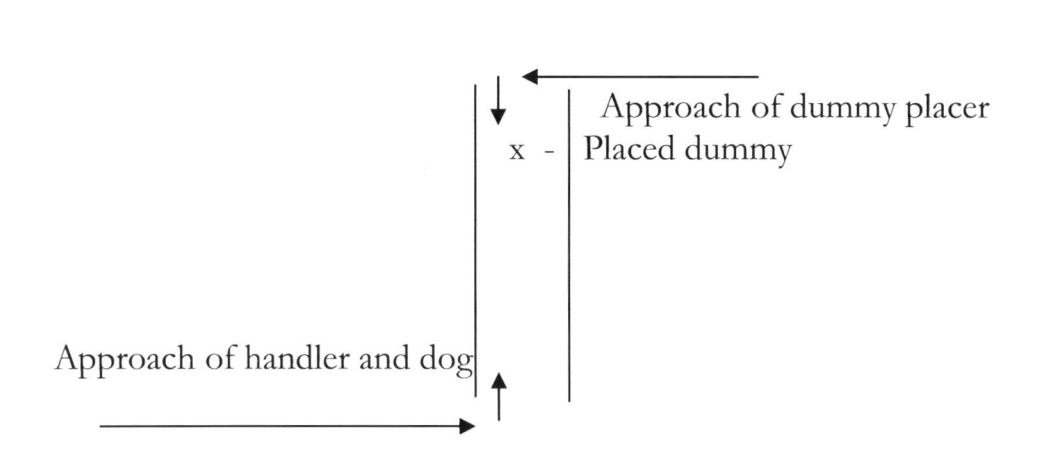

```
            ↓  ←────────
         ┌──┤    Approach of dummy placer
      x -│      Placed dummy
         │
         │
Approach of handler and dog│
─────────────────────────→ ↑
```

The reason for placing the dummy in this way is to guard against a dog following the scent left by ourselves or another person, who places the dummy. The dog would then be tracking, and we want the dog to understand he should go in the direction he is sent rather than go on scent. Do not let the dog watch either the dummy placer, or the dummy being placed so keep well out of the way whilst this is being done.

After the dummy is placed, approach the area with the dog at heel and when at a suitable, short distance away from the placed dummy, line the dog up as usual and give the 'go back' command.

Hopefully your dog will leave your side and find the dummy relatively quickly. If a dog is hesitant, run with the dog, all the way, if necessary, without repeating the command. Let the dog find, and pick up the dummy, and then run back with him to your starting position whilst the dummy thrower places another dummy in exactly the same place. You can then try again and will probably find the dog will do it himself. If not, just encourage, setting up the exercise several times and then do no more until trying again in a day or two's time.

On subsequent training sessions you can try placing the dummy at a greater distance and once the dog is going out confidently on his own, the dummy can be placed in cover so he has to hunt on the 'hie lost' command once he gets to the correct area.

You will find you have more success, and the dog will gain more confidence, if you keep to straight lines using either a track or hedge line. Do not be tempted to push things along too quickly by sending the dog diagonally across a field, or into a wood, or dense cover until you are certain the dog is confident, and understands what is required. Then you can try short diagonal lines, but it is important to make sure that you do not send the dog the distance, to start with, which you had previously built up on a track or similar straight line.

Starting diagonal lines is sometimes best achieved by sending the dog to something like a bush, a corner of a field, a large area of higher grass or any other distinctive feature. Using the corner of a field is useful. You can then stand out in the field with the dog and send him diagonally to the corner. Using something to aim for in these ways not only helps the dog, but helps the handler remember where the dummy is too!

(z) Hand signals

It is important to make sure that hand signals are clear and the body outline is changed by holding the arm well above the head.

This position of dog and handler is the starting point for many exercises. The hand signal, together with a 'stop' whistle, means to the dog *'sit, or continue sitting, and look at me because I am going to tell you what to do next'*. Once the dog is looking at the handler the next command could be a 'go back', a 'get on' or a recall command.

When sitting at a distance, the dog should remain steady and should focus on the handler, waiting to be told what to do.

The use of the right or left hand and arm, together with the 'stop' whistle, is an indication to the dog which direction they are to be sent next, or which direction the dummy or bird is located.

(Photographs: Paul Rawlings)

CHAPTER TWENTY-TWO

Development of direction work.

I think that when novice handlers in particular, arrive at the point of putting numerous training aspects together and they witness their dog actually doing a variety of things, totally on command, and totally in the control of their handler that there is a magical feel to everything. All the component parts, having been manufactured separately, suddenly start being put together to form a recognisable structure.

Even though I have been through this stage numerous times myself, as well as taught and witnessed this with hundreds of others, I have never lost the feeling of thinking it is magical. It still gives me a thrill to watch a young dog developing and wanting to do things just for me, or to witness dogs, which arrived in class just a few months previously as raw but enthusiastic puppies, working for their handlers in ways that most of the handlers never thought possible.

I think we should all feel the joy of this relationship and never forget how special it is and remember we are just part of, hopefully, an everlasting chain made up of links of the partnership of person and dog working together. This chain has been growing and developing for thousands of years. I believe we have a duty to ensure our contribution to this chain will not jeopardise further links being added for thousands of years hence. We should value and see the magic in the relationship we form with each and every dog we are privileged to own. Each of them gives us so much; sadly, we give them less in return but fortunately they ask for little. This is why a 'good boy' goes such a long way and is such a small price for us to pay.

By the time the magic moments have arrived, you will have taught your dog nearly everything he needs to know regarding the basic foundations. The construction is complete, you have taken control.

The following ideas and exercises are designed to further the process of putting two and two together and now they really make five, because the whole is greater than its component parts!

The three card trick.

This exercise is not really a 'trick' but just a way to test and see if your dog understands the directional commands learnt so far.

You should not try this until your dog is steady, knows, and responds instantly, to the 'go back' command and also knows, and responds instantly, to the 'get on' and 'recall' commands. It is also preferable if your dog is going for marks swiftly and keenly with no problems concerning steadiness, returning to you, or the subsequent present.

The goal is to have your dog in a sit position, at a distance from you, to throw three dummies; one behind, one to the left and one to the right of the dog and for the dog to go, on command, to retrieve a dummy of *your* choice, ignoring all other dummies.

Training.

You will eventually need three dummies for the exercise.

Position your dog in a sit and then go and stand facing your dog, about 6 paces away. To begin, use only 2 dummies. Throw one dummy over the dog's head (try not to hit the dog) to land behind the dog, slightly on the right hand side, as you look at it. Throw the other dummy to your left, to land in a straight line with the dog but at a further distance from the dog than the back dummy.

Taking Control

```
                        X   (back dummy)


X (Side dummy)          D (dog)




                        H (handler)
```

Your dog has never experienced this before so you will need to repeat your sit commands, either verbally or with the whistle whilst you throw the dummies and ensure your dog does not move. You also want to prevent the dog going wrong and therefore need to plan your part in this exercise carefully.

The first consideration needs to be your hand signals. You have been teaching the dog that the use of your left arm or your right arm is important in relation to where the dog has to go. For a 'go back' he has to turn round and go away from you either slightly left, if you use your left hand, or slightly right, if you use your right hand. For a 'get on' he has to go directly to his left, if you use your right hand, or directly to his right, if you use your left hand.

For this exercise therefore, you need to set it up so that your dog will do it correctly and therefore learn from this!

You see on the diagram that the back dummy is situated slightly right of the dog and much closer to the dog than the dummy on the left side. This is deliberate!

You are going to send the dog back first, so the last thing you would want to do, is to have to use your left hand because there is also a dummy on the left, to the side. The dog will also concentrate on the last dummy thrown, which is on the left and a keen dog may well misinterpret what you want him to do. If he goes for the left dummy, you will have taught him nothing, other than to disobey you.

Eventually your dog should be able to do a 'go back' and a 'get on' in any direction, even when there are other dummies placed at the back, left or right, but not at this stage!

So to begin: throw the back dummy and then throw the side dummy. Remember that the dog will concentrate on the last dummy thrown, which is the side dummy. You need to get the dog's attention back to you after throwing the dummies, so blow your stop whistle (to mean 'continue sitting and watch me because I am going to tell you what to do').

Use your right hand and arm when you give this whistle command because you are going to send the dog for the back dummy, which is slightly right of the dog. When the dog looks at you, drop your arm and then say 'good boy' (for looking at you) keep the dog looking at you and then give the 'go back' verbal and hand signal command. Hopefully, the dog will turn and go back to retrieve the dummy because he knows this command.

When the dog returns to you and has presented the dummy, put the dog on a sit and you go and pick up the remaining dummy from the left.

Problems.

- 🐾 The most likely problem, is that the dog, despite what you may be saying and doing, will go to retrieve the left hand dummy. If you have someone with you, try and get the other person to pick up the dummy before the dog can retrieve it. If you are alone, try and stop the dog *before* he reaches the dummy either by saying 'no', 'leave it' or blowing your stop whistle. If the dog obeys this command, he should be praised and you should then pick up the dummies. You can then return to the dog, reposition him exactly as before and try again.

- If the dog has retrieved the wrong dummy, take it from him but do not praise him. Then reposition him exactly as before. This time throw the left hand dummy first, then the back dummy. In this way the dog should concentrate on the back dummy. If he retrieves this one correctly, try again on the original exercise.

If there are any problems it is best to try the exercise up to 3 times and then take the dog home to think before trying again a few days later. It is important to keep trying, for however long it takes, before moving on as below when the dog has learned to do it correctly.

Next, sit the dog up as before and throw the dummies again but throw the left dummy first, fairly close to the dog, followed by the back dummy at a greater distance.

You should now send the dog for the left dummy, with a 'get on' command; following the same procedure as before but using your left hand and arm to give the stop whistle command initially. If the dog retrieves the left hand dummy correctly, sit the dog up, you go and pick up the back dummy, and then do no more on that session. Let the dog think about this new exercise and it will then be time to take things a little further on subsequent training sessions.

You have now successfully commanded your dog to retrieve a dummy of your choice, twice, even though there was another dummy available on each occasion, which he *could* have retrieved, so be pleased with yourself and be proud of your dog. Wait a day or two before going further with this exercise and let the dog assimilate the new information.

With all these progressions it is important to remember to reposition the dog after each retrieve, in the same place, before sending the dog for another dummy. Progress can then be made as follows:

- 🐾 Throw the back dummy, slightly to the left and one dummy out to the right. Send the dog for the back dummy, using your left hand and arm. After the dog has retrieved and presented the dummy, you should go and pick up the remaining dummy.
- 🐾 Next, reposition the dog and throw a dummy to the right, then a dummy to the back and send the dog out for the right hand dummy. Afterwards, you pick up the remaining dummy.
- 🐾 You can then begin to throw other dummies back again, to the place from which the dummy has already been retrieved. So, throw 2 dummies to begin and when the dog has retrieved the first, reposition him, throw another dummy to the place from where the dog has already retrieved and then send him for the dummy remaining of the first two. When he has retrieved this dummy, you should pick up the last dummy thrown as a replacement.
- 🐾 Throw the back dummy directly behind the dog and then throw a dummy to the left and one to the right. Send the dog for the back dummy, using the left hand and arm. Repeat by throwing a dummy out to the left, then one to the right followed by one to the back. Send the dog for the left hand dummy. Repeat by throwing a dummy out to the right, then one to the left, followed by one to the back. Send the dog for the right hand dummy. You pick up the remaining dummies on each occasion.
- 🐾 Replacing dummies already retrieved, can then be done when three dummies are thrown initially.

At this stage, your dog will have successfully retrieved a dummy of your choice from any of the three directions, even though there were another two dummies out which he could have retrieved.

You will have built up slowly and always sent your dog for the first dummy thrown, firstly when it was the first of two and secondly, when it was the first of three.

You can now begin to put in a few variations: send the dog for a dummy thrown second or third in the order; after the dog has retrieved one dummy, reposition the dog in the centre and send him for one and later two of the remaining dummies; reposition the dog and recall him then send him on a 'go back' from your side after the left and right hand dummies have been picked; turn the exercise into a 4 card trick by throwing the three dummies as usual and adding a 4th dummy, thrown a few yards in front of your dog.

Try as many variations as you can and in as many different places as you can find, so that the dog learns what the commands mean in practice, in different locations and on different terrain. Throw the dummies into cover on some occasions or have one in cover, which you want, and one fairly close in the open, which you do not want.

Once the dog is responding well and able to go in whichever direction you send him, start increasing the distances involved. In the beginning, start to increase the distance between yourself and the dog, then increase the distance between the dog and the dummies.

You are now handling your dog at distance and your dog is learning that you are still in control, even when he is at a great distance from you.

Marks and blinds

The magic square.

Take the dog to a training area where you have an open space with little cover or distractions and sit your dog up in the open in a similar way to when you were teaching the 'get on' command.

You need to define a large square, in your mind or use geographical features for some of the sides, such as a wall or fence for side one, trees or pathways for another side. With your dog positioned in the middle of side 1 of your square, throw a dummy to the left and one to the right. Send the dog to retrieve the left hand dummy. When that dummy is retrieved, leave the right hand dummy where it is and reposition your dog in the middle of the second side of your square – working clockwise. Throw a dummy to the right but send the dog for the left hand dummy, which was the dummy remaining after the first retrieve. When that dummy is retrieved, reposition the dog in the middle of the third side of the square and continue the exercise until 4 sides have been completed.

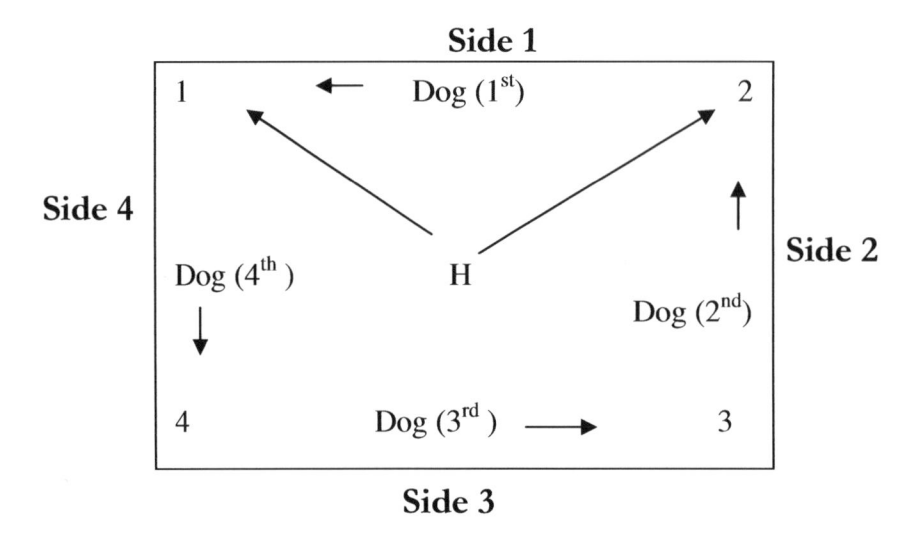

In this way your dog will have completed 4 semi blinds with a distraction of a mark on each occasion. Progress can then be made as follows:

- Try the exercise in a similar way but throw a dummy to the right and then to the left. Send the dog going for the right hand dummy first and then move round the square anti clockwise.
- Go to the same location but leave the dog in the car. Go and place out 4 dummies in the same places as you threw them previously, which is one dummy in each corner of the square. Go and get the dog and position him as before. The only difference with this is that the dog will not see you throw any dummies. Send him either for the left hand dummy first, and

work clockwise round the square; or send him for the right hand dummy first and work anti-clockwise round the square.
- Using blinds as above, do the same exercise by putting the blinds in the corners, and then throw a diversionary mark on occasions, which the dog should not retrieve.

Once the dog has managed these exercises, further progress can be made as follows:

- Set up blinds on and over water, through hedges and over small jumps.
- Try and build up distance gradually and attempt to get your dog going out on a straight line at speed, further and therefore for longer. This can sometimes only be achieved a yard at a time. Do not always do long distances however; now and again do a short distance too.
- Gradually increase the degree of difficulty and introduce rough cover, woodland, reeds and anything you can find to increase your dogs' experience and confidence.
- Introduce your dog gradually to following a line of scent – tennis balls are useful for this as you can roll a ball down a slope and watch your dog following the line. Rub a dummy on the ground in a circle and then drag the dummy over the ground a short distance before leaving it.
- Have a dummy thrown in front of you and your dog, whilst he is in the heel position on a sit. Then, do an about turn with the dog at heel, stop and send the dog in the opposite direction ('go back' command) for an already placed, short blind.
- This last exercise is called a blind with a distraction. The distraction is the mark in front, and to begin it is better for you to pick up this dummy after the dog has successfully retrieved the blind. Later you can send the dog for the mark after he has retrieved the blind in which case it will be a double retrieve – a mark with a blind. This helps the dog remember where dummies are located, for a longer period of time. Do not always send the dog for the mark, sometimes send another

dog, sometimes pick it up yourself and sometimes get the dummy thrower to pick it up.

All these exercises help the dog to understand: he must go in the direction you send him; he must only retrieve the item you tell him to retrieve and just because he has seen something, it does not always follow that he will retrieve it.

Start to increase distance on marks which you get others to throw for you. Do it gradually but do not always use long distances, so put shorter marks in on occasions. It is important to teach the dog to judge distances accurately and he will only be able to do this if you give him opportunities to learn how to do it. Vary distances!

It is also vital at this stage to make a rule for yourself; if your dog does not go straight to the fall on a mark, hunt if necessary for a short while in the correct place, and return to you immediately with the dummy, *that you recall the dog*. Ask the dummy thrower to pick up the dummy and then start again exactly the same. Do not be tempted to try and handle your dog and help him whilst he is out there. (See Marked retrieves) The best help you can give him is to call him back, set up the exercise again in exactly the same way, and let him learn for himself.

It is the dog's job to mark the fall and he must learn that if he does not go straight there and find the dummy or bird, he does not get it. Failing to recall the dog at this stage, results in you teaching the dog that he does not need to concentrate on the fall because you will do that bit and then help him. You do not want him to learn this, so it is your responsibility to make sure he is not given the opportunity to learn anything which is undesirable from your point of view.

Dogs which are poor markers can be *made* and they are made this way frequently by handlers doing some or all of the following:

- Allowing the dog to go a long way from the fall, without recalling the dog. It is not good enough that the dog goes everywhere but the fall, hunts inappropriately and somehow finds the dummy in the last place he hunts.
- Handlers trying to redirect the dog if it fails to go straight to the correct area.
- Handlers saying 'mark' thus getting the attention of the dog on themselves instead of saying nothing and letting the dog pay attention to whoever is saying 'mark', or focussing on the direction of a shot, or watching the dummy being thrown.
- On double retrieves, the handler telling the dog 'leave it' when the 'mark' is thrown before sending the dog for a blind. Many dogs will take the 'leave it' command to mean 'don't you dare touch that dummy *ever*'. If you want the mark retrieved by the dog after he has retrieved the blind, some dogs will not go anywhere near it. A 'leave it' command should not be necessary at this stage because you have taken control. The dog has also learnt to control himself and understands that *sit means sit no matter what……………….!*
- If a shot noise is used on a marked retrieve, you should also beware, of anyone firing and throwing dummies incorrectly. By this I mean that the shot should be fired first, and then the dummy thrown. In this way, the dog is alerted by the sound of the shot and then is able to see the fall of the dummy. It is surprising how many people do this the wrong way round, that is, they will throw the dummy and *then* fire the shot. By the time the dog looks towards the shot, he has missed seeing the dummy. This can create a poor marking dog if it happens too frequently. It should never happen in training. It would never happen when on a shoot because there is no way a bird can land, shot on the ground, *before* the gun is fired.

None of the above is desirable and it is better to start by *not* doing any of the things which create problems. This is the responsibility of the handler. Unfortunately, if the handler develops these problems and habits, it is the dog which will show the symptoms.

The cure for the dog is painful, not physically, but as he must be re-trained on these matters it will have to involve some kind of hardship for him if only because he will not understand.

This is extremely unfair on the dog! He has been taught and therefore learned a variety of habits, doing his best to achieve what the handler wanted whereas the handler did not really want these things at all.

You should therefore do your best to avoid putting your dog through a rehabilitation programme which may involve months of withdrawal agonies! A re-trained dog is a bit like a broken cup. We can stick it together with glue so that it looks perfect afterwards, it will hold tea adequately but, under pressure and when you least expect it, the cup will start leaking or disintegrate completely.

The solution is not to damage it in the first place!

We all get into habits and use body language of which we are unaware. If you want to avoid too many bad habits creeping in, get someone to watch you and ask them to be honest in saying what they see! It may surprise you!

It will be useful to understand however, why your dog may be doing or not doing something or behaving in a way you feel is inappropriate. You should ask yourself the question, 'what am I doing or not doing which has made the dog behave in this way?' You should not assume that the dog is deliberately going against your teaching or wishes. We rarely have stupid dogs, despite what we may sometimes believe, and there is usually something we have done or not done which has created a symptom in the dog.

Conclusion

By the time you and your dog get to the end of everything contained in *'Taking Control'*, all the commands your dog will need to understand, have now been taught although these, in most cases have been taught using set exercises. Gundogs are perhaps unique in the sphere of dog training in that for most other competition or assessment disciplines such as, for example obedience, agility, flyball and Good Citizen, the exercises taught, are the ones which the dogs will demonstrate in competition or a test situation in almost the same format. In other words, what they are taught is what they will need to demonstrate.

The training exercises taught to gundogs are simply a means to an end, or the tools which we use to create an end product for the shooting field. Apart from perhaps Puppy Gundog working tests, dogs are not required to demonstrate exercises as such, but to demonstrate in a variety of settings, that they are steady, will obey a variety of commands used to help in a retrieving situation as well as being able to demonstrate a variety of skills concerning ability to negotiate obstacles including water. All these aspects of well-rounded retrieving gundogs have only one goal, which is that of retrieving dead and wounded birds efficiently and without disrupting anything or anybody else, in the process.

Further work needs to be completed to ensure that your dog actually understands commands and that you have not, inadvertently, taught him to perform only an exercise.

This may not be clear to novice handlers but unless you ensure that, for example, you teach the dog that a particular command must be obeyed here, there and everywhere, it is possible that a dog learns only that the command must be obeyed in the training group, or one area where you do most of your training, or, in some cases, only when there is a training instructor present.

No person and dog partnership will manage to get through all the stages of training without any problems. People and dogs are unique and they all have their own blends of personality, capabilities, skills, and attributes. They all learn at different rates and whereas for some, one training concept may be difficult to understand, learn and master, another aspect may be taught, learnt and become expert, within minutes.

Training should not be seen as a race and although it is difficult not to compare your own puppy with another, it is important to remember that as long as you carry on doing all the right things in the correct order, you and your dog will succeed.

Every person and every dog has a different rate of learning and it is not possible to give time scales for training, as much depends also on the amount of time you have available for teaching your dog and how long each person and dog partnership take to grasp a particular concept. If you start with your puppy around 10 weeks of age with the first introduction to the lead; work consistently through each aspect of training, make sure you do not add a new piece of training until you are sure your dog understands what he has already been taught, then a dog of between 10 to 12 months will hopefully have learned all the desired basics.

Some dogs will have learned these before 10 months, some may take longer than a year but at some point around the age of 1 year, your dog will be ready to begin using the skills learned in a variety of new ways, which may include introduction to aspects associated with a shoot day.

I am not advocating that you immediately take your puppy to a shoot and then expect him to do everything learned in training because, as with everything new, at each step you should only add one new factor at a time. The first time a dog goes to a shoot it will be sufficient if the dog is able to sit by your side and watch a drive, which is not too exciting!

What I like to do, is to sit a puppy up by my side and let him experience the birds flying and the sound of the guns and perhaps watch a few birds being shot and fall to the ground. Plan this first experience so that if possible, you are within sight of the guns, but quite a distance behind them. I like to take a puppy dummy in my pocket and when the drive has finished, and if the opportunity presents itself, perhaps go and pick up a shot bird myself and then give my puppy a simple marked retrieve using the dummy. That is usually sufficient for most dogs for their first experience and it is better at that stage to put your dog back in the car and do no more on that occasion.

With particularly mature dogs, and if you have managed to try your dog previously on a small item of cold game then you could perhaps try the dog on one shot bird on their first shoot. You should make sure the bird is dead. Many dogs will not mind at this stage if the bird is still alive, but some dogs can be put off for a long time if their first experience is with a live bird.

If a suitable bird is available, and if the opportunity arises, then send your dog for the bird but be ready to go with the dog, if necessary to encourage. If your dog does pick up the bird, be happy and do not be tempted to do any more other than give the dog another retrieve using your dummy.

It is important to make sure the dog understands that he must still retrieve a dummy, when commanded, even though he has retrieved a warm, freshly shot bird. There are some dogs which get a little difficult when they have had game in their mouth and it is important for you to re-establish your leadership position so that the dog understands that if you command him to retrieve anything, then that is his job, no questions asked, and he cannot choose!

What you have managed to teach the dog so far, are the basics. You have formed the foundations and created a framework. There is more, but for now you have managed to *take control*. You should also have learned *how and why,* control is not only desirable, but essential, for the partnership between you and your dog to work effectively.

You and your dog will need to make more progress, it is almost a never ending process; you need to be able to further your control, use the control you have taken effectively, and learn how to maintain control for the rest of the lifetime together with your dog.

Remember that appropriate praise is the most effective teaching tool you possess and remember too that your dog will work for you after you have taught him what he is to do, because he accepts you are his pack leader.

Every dog gives so much. Every dog asks for so little in return.

A smile, a 'good boy' and a pat on the head, means everything to the dog. This is all he requires in terms of a salary. Do not disappoint him!

Good luck on your journey of discovery with your dog and I hope you have enjoyed *'Taking Control'* as much as your dog will appreciate having a valued leader at the end.

The journey is not yet over, you will need to take *'Further Control'* to add some polish to the structure already assembled but your hard work has been accomplished and I hope the future will hold many years of treasured moments for you both.

Also by Anthea Lawrence:

Respect & Leadership in dog training
& related articles

Anthea Lawrence

(Photograph: Nigel Haines)

Available from www.trafford.com

ISBN 1-4120-9942-0

Printed in Great Britain
by Amazon.co.uk, Ltd.,
Marston Gate.